Break Free!

Take Control of Your Money Today for a Better Tomorrow

By Rod and Cheryl Kuratomi

INTRODUCTION

Congratulations! In buying this book, you have taken the first step to regain and/or secure your financial freedom. This book contains critical basic information which is not taught to most people in school. We are bombarded from birth with advertising and things to spend our money on, but not on how to save, manage, and invest our money.

Here are a few common problems that may sound too familiar to you:

- Credit cards are maxed out (Spending to the credit limit)
- Unable to save money (Savings account is low or zero)
- Live paycheck to paycheck (Always waiting for payday)
- Personal lives and relationships are a wreck due to poor financial decisions (You and your partner are always fighting about money)
- Can't afford to buy your own home (Perpetual renters)
- Can't balance a checkbook (Never educated on how important it is or never took the time to learn)
- Can't create a simple budget (What's a budget? Isn't that for the government?)
- Never seem to have enough cash (Isn't that what credit cards are for? No!)
- Lifestyle does not match income (To the educated observer, but not to the person making the mistakes!)

- Collections letters and phone calls are a regular occurrence (Annoying and stressful!)

I am just an average guy who had an average job making an average wage and living in an expensive city (Los Angeles). What is not average about me is that I was able to retire at age 54 and live comfortably. I am going to teach you how to manage your finances so that you too can enjoy your life to the fullest. You will learn how to create a budget, effectively manage your debt, and improve your financial health, regardless of your financial situation. If this sort of freedom sounds good to you, read on!

I obtained my first credit card and checking account when I was 18 years old and in college. I had no idea how to balance a checkbook. I did not know the ramifications of charging items to my credit card when I could not afford to pay the monthly balance in full. Many lessons found in this book were learned from my own mistakes and by watching those around me make poor financial decisions. By reading this book and applying the information to your own life, you will be able to avoid many of the financial pitfalls which affect most people. If you have already fallen off the cliff, this book can provide you with the information necessary to rescue yourself. Many financial mistakes are life changing and difficult to recover from at best, disastrous at worst.

This book is going to assume you know nothing about finance. It will start with the most basic concepts, but I promise that no matter your level of knowledge, you will learn something. Hopefully, the reading will be worthwhile and entertaining, as it contains examples we can all relate to or know someone who is in the same predicament. Sometimes we can see the mistakes others make without seeing mistakes we have made ourselves. This book will resonate with most people, as we have all made at least some of these mistakes at some point in our lives. If you are a young person, this book can help you prevent money problems before they happen. If you are older and in debt, this book can help you to improve your financial situation and help you to regain your financial freedom.

The majority of people in the United States need financial help! Often, it's not that people need more money, but rather that they need to better manage the money they do have. They need to learn how to get out of debt, or better yet, how to not get into debt in the first place.

Many of us do not understand the importance of basic financial knowledge. With the help of this book, you will be better able to understand the root of your problems and discover some solutions to your financial woes. If you are young and don't have financial problems yet, this book can help you to remain problem free. The end result will be a healthier, happier life (stress kills!).

Many financial problems could have been avoided if we had learned how to manage money early on in school, when we were growing up. Public schools are great about teaching history, language, science, art, math, and sports, but often neglect one thing everyone needs: Basic knowledge about how to better handle money. Finance is not a required class and is not offered in many schools. I spent countless hours as a youth studying things I never used in later life. I use personal finance every day, and the only math I need for this is how to add, subtract, multiply, and divide. Unless you are an engineer or scientist, you will probably never need the calculus or algebra you struggled with as a kid growing up.

It is said that money can't buy you happiness, but the lack of money or the inability to manage it properly is a guarantee to a life full of unhappiness. Remember, financial problems are one of the main reasons that couples fight.

It was my goal to write a book that contains the basic knowledge that every young person and adult needs to know but was never taught. By reading this book, you will be able to avoid some of the pitfalls that come not from stupidity, but rather from lack of basic knowledge. Sometimes we don't know what we don't know because we were never taught! It's an oversight in the education system. I worked in the healthcare field with many doctors. Did you know that many doctors have their own medical practice which is a business, but business and finance are not a required part of their extensive education? As a result, many doctors make a lot of money but are just as much in debt, and sometimes more so, than the average person. Making more money "qualifies" them to be able to manage (or rather, mis-manage) more debt in the eyes of banks or other financial institutions.

There are professionals who are so much in debt that if they were unable to work for some reason, they would lose everything in only a few months. I know a few doctors that have "trophy" wives who don't work but are experts at shopping and spending money. On the other hand, there are people with a good grasp of basic financial fundamentals who have average jobs and are able to retire when they are middle aged, because of good money management and because they spend within their means. I know a person who works in a hospital in a fairly low-paying job. She contributed the maximum allowed to her retirement plan since she was young, invested wisely, and now has a retirement portfolio worth $3.8 million.

She did this with a job that paid less than $20 per hour for most of her career. Last year, income from her retirement investments alone made her $200,000! I don't know about you, but I could live well on $200,000 a year. Sometimes, rich people don't work for their money; they let their money work for them.

Back in 1982, my old boss had a son, Marc, who was an ear, nose, and throat surgeon. Marc was making hundreds of thousands of dollars a year. In fact, he was a pioneer of an anti-snore surgical procedure. At the time, I was a 20-year-old college student working part time for his father, making $8 an hour as an electronics technician. One day Marc said to me, "I drive a fancy car and live in a nice house in a beach community, but you know what? At the end of the month, I have the same amount of money left in my wallet as you do." What a revelation!

Get ready to learn the information you need which can lead to getting your finances under control, or better yet, to prevent your finances from getting out of control in the first place. If you live a financially responsible life, this book can help you to retire early and live off your investment income or be able to save enough money to open your own business and become financially independent.

Acknowledgement

I would like to dedicate this book to my wife Cheryl. Without her vision and inspiration, early retirement would not have been possible. Sometimes when people retire, they go back to work because spending extended periods of time with their life partner is too difficult. We are not like those couples. One reason we retired early is that we realize life is short. We want to spend time together while we are still healthy enough to travel, have fun, and enjoy life. Our relationship is a match made in heaven, I will never take my wife nor our relationship for granted, and I appreciate every single moment we have together. If the next 30 years go by as fast as the last 30 years, our lives on this Earth will be over in a blink of an eye. Notice how the weeks and years go by faster as we age? There is a saying, "Life is like a roll of toilet paper. As the roll is used up, it spins faster and runs out more quickly"!

Make the best of your life. Our time on Earth is very limited, and the only life we are sure about and have control over is the current one. It is my hope that you can follow the advice and lessons in this book and that you find financial freedom. This freedom will bring joy and happiness back into your life. Money usually can't buy happiness, but it can get you out of a whole lot of unhappiness if you don't have enough of it to live on.

I also want to thank my karate instructor and adopted father, Soke Takayuki Kubota of the International Karate Association. The discipline I learned through his karate teachings enabled me to be the person I am today. My sister told me that if it was not for Master Kubota, by now I would have been dead or in jail! Thank you, Soke!

I started to write this book on my own, but as I progressed, my wife ended up contributing a great deal, so in the end, the book was written by both of us.

Thank you also to my daughter Traci (AKA The Financial MBA Wizard), who did the initial editing. Traci's birth prompted me to be responsible. I learned that the love for our children far outweigh love for ourselves, and it gives our lives much greater purpose. My daughter's birth gave me the drive I needed to get my financial affairs in order.

We hope you learn and enjoy!

TABLE OF CONTENTS

Introduction

Preface

Acknowledgement

- Refinancing to Obtain Cash for Other Items

- Get it in Writing

In the next few chapters, I will make references to a few fictitious characters in the book. They are two couples: Dan and Danielle Disaster, who spend like there is no tomorrow, and their counterparts, Frank and Francine Frugal, who make all the smart financial decisions. There are many real-life Dan and Danielle Disasters in the world, but few Frank and Francine Frugals. It is my hope that by the end of this book, you can transform yourself into a Frugal and avoid the mistakes made by the Disasters.

CHAPTER 1
BASIC PREMISE OF FINANCE

Believe it or not, it is not Rocket Science!

The most basic premise is that you have income (plus) and expenses (minus). The goal to have the plus number be greater than the minus number at the end of each month. Sounds simple, right? Let's look at some examples of common mistakes made by Dan and Danielle Disaster, and smart moves made by Frank and Francine Frugal.

Dan and Danielle Disaster always spend more than they make. Their credit cards are maxed out, and the telephone rings day and night from creditors and collectors trying to get money owed to them. As a result, Dan and Danielle fight constantly and blame each other for their problems. On the other hand, Frank and Francine Frugal never spend more than they make, which allows them to save money. Frank and Francine are young, only in their early 30's, but are already well on their way to saving for retirement. Dan and Danielle are doomed to work far past retirement age just to survive. Frank and Francine are on track to retire ten years early and will enjoy their retirement in leisure and travel. The Frugals know too many of their parents' friends who retired late in life and then died shortly after retirement; they did not live long enough to enjoy retirement. Wouldn't you rather be like the Frugals?

CHAPTER 2
DISCIPLINE AND SPENDING

People today live in an instant-gratification society. If we want something, we buy it NOW. If we want to do something, we do it NOW. We don't take time to figure out the costs or the consequences of our actions and decisions. We are impulsive! I blame society as a whole for brainwashing us to be consumers. Just look at television and the internet and see that we are constantly bombarded with advertisements and emails, encouraging us to spend our hard-earned cash.

The Disaster Family's Destructive Habits

The Disasters always get the latest smartphones. It's easy. The vendor will allow them to pay for the phones in monthly installments and with no interest if they sign a two-year contract. So what if the monthly payments are for two years? So what, you say? The Disasters think they can afford $42 a month, no problem! At $42 per month per phone, that's more than $1,000 per year! Add insurance for $9 per month, making the monthly payment per smartphone $51 each. Add a large data plan for additional $100 a month, or $1,200 annually. That bumps up the annual cost to over $1,800 each! For the two-year contract, the Disasters will spend over $3,600 on their two smartphones. Get a new phone every two years, and that expense never goes away.

Dan also bought a new sports car. It's awesome! He will look so cool driving his new wheels, and all of his friends and family will be envious. So what if the payments are $600 a month for seven years? He can afford it. Heck, it's only a few thousand dollars for the down payment and only a few percent in interest a year. What's the big deal? The big deal is that Dan has other expenses related to the car which he did not take into consideration, such as insurance and maintenance. The insurance for a sports car can easily be 10% to 20% more than a mainstream sedan, and maintenance for a sports car typically costs more as well. The car expenses added up and combined with their other expenses exceeded the Disasters' family income. This is where trouble starts. Including the down payment, monthly payments (which include interest on the loan), insurance, maintenance, car registration, and other costs, the car which started out as "only $600 a month" (over $50,000 over seven years) will eventually cost Dan a total of $60,000 to $70,000 or more.

Oh, and Danielle leases a new BMW every two years. Her car cost "only" a $5,000 down payment and a little over $400 a month. This brings the Disaster family monthly car payments up to $1,000 per month!

In the 1980's when I worked my wealthy boss, Phil, he complained that an oil change for his Mercedes Benz cost over $400 (something about how the oil injectors on his 450SL sedan had to be changed with every oil change). It was then I learned that anyone can buy an expensive car if they save the money; however, you have to be rich to maintain it.

Frank Frugal's Car Savings

Frugal Frank, on the other hand, has driven the same economy car for seven years now. He bought a reliable little Honda which costs him very little to maintain, and it gets great gas mileage. Frank paid cash for the car with his savings, saving more money since he doesn't pay interest on a car loan. He plans on driving the car until it is no longer cost effective to repair. He expects this will probably be another five to seven years.

Frank's car may not look as cool as Dan's sports car, but it cost Frank a fraction of Dan's car to purchase, insure, and maintain. Frank's car gets great gas mileage which saves him even more money. Guess what? Frank can do a lot more with his Honda than Dan can do with his sports car (except impress others as much). He can carry more passengers, and the trunk is bigger. If Dan wants to have more than one passenger, he has to borrow his wife's BMW. Oh, and Francine does not have a car, as Frank and Francine carpool. By not owning a second car, the Frugal family saves each year on insurance, maintenance, fuel, and car registration. Who is the financial winner?

Shopping, Anyone?

Shopping can be an addiction. Dan and Danielle Disaster always have the latest trendy clothes and shoes. Francine Frugal looks for sales at the local department store. She always looks good but does not care for the extra cost of designer label clothing. Frank is happy wearing his jeans and flannel shirts because they are super comfortable.

Dan loves luxury watches and owns a Rolex and several other expensive wristwatches. Frank has worn the same Casio watch for the last ten years. It keeps perfect time and the battery lasts ten years. Dan has to get his Rolex serviced every five years at a cost of over $500 each time.

Danielle can't pass up a sale and has boxes and boxes of new stuff that she has never used. She has so much stuff still new in the box that she has forgotten exactly what she bought, so she buys more stuff that she doesn't need.

Frank and Francine, on the other hand, only buy what they will actually use. They purchase what they need, but neither goes for the latest fashion trend nor sees the need to buy the latest electronic gadgets. Frank and Francine make a bit of a sacrifice, but they know that financial freedom is worth every cent saved.

Story of A Real Dan Disaster

I have friends who were newly married (we'll call them Bill and Cindy). Bill recently completed trade school to be an electrician and now has debt for the tuition. Since he does not have his own 'contractor's license, he found a low-paying job as an apprentice. He just bought a new sports car which cost around $35,000. For a guy who owes a lot of money for his education and makes a low wage, that purchase was a big mistake. His wife also has a low-paying job but has a taste for the finer things in life. She recently spent $5,000 on a dining room set. Now, they are looking for a house and have come to the realization that they don't have enough money for the down payment! The debt incurred for the trade school, a new car, and a new dining room set alone will have them tapped out financially for years, and I don't think they have figured it out yet. The latest news? His wife is now pregnant, and they have no place to live to call their own. They have no clue what it costs to raise a child and buy a house. This is one of the true-life stories which pushed me to write this book. If I have many friends who have made big financial mistakes so early in life, I'm sure there are thousands just like them in the good old USA. Credit is far too easy to obtain, to the detriment of the uninformed public. There are thousands of Dan and Danielle Disasters out there, and some don't even know they have a problem -- yet.

CHAPTER 3
BANK ACCOUNTS

OK, this is basic stuff. But bear with me, as I am trying to educate both the young as well as the old. I promise that you more experienced men and women will learn something later in the book.

There are many types of bank accounts. I will keep it simple and talk about the two basics types, savings accounts and checking accounts. You can access both savings and checking accounts from an automated teller machine (ATM), in person, or online via computer or smart device, depending on your bank. This is standard for all major banks today.

<u>Savings Account</u>

A savings account is a bank account designated for "savings". It is usually used to set aside money and save it for a future expense. The bank will usually pay you a very small amount of interest every month; as of this writing, the interest is often less than 1% annually. A savings account may also be "linked" to your checking account, which makes it easier to move money back and forth between the accounts, for reasons outlined below. Some savings accounts are moving toward "negative" interest, where you actually have to pay the bank to hold your money! This is a side effect of our artificially low interest rates, which further takes away the incentive for people to save money.

Checking Account

A checking account is a bank account which provides a convenient way for you to give money to someone else or to make payments. (More on writing a check later!) You can also make payments electronically, which we will cover later. There are Apps for smartphones and other electronic devices which allow you to perform banking functions easily. Checking accounts often charge a monthly fee, which appears on your monthly statement. Many banks will offer a free checking account if you maintain a certain amount of money (a balance) in your savings and/or checking account or if your employer deposits your paycheck directly into your bank account ("direct deposit").

Many people like to keep only a minimum amount of money in their checking account. This way, if someone tries to steal money from the checking account, the loss will be minimized. For example, say someone stole your checkbook and forged a check for $1000, but you have only $100 in the account. You would not lose the $1000 because the money is not available in the checking account. The way this works is that you keep money in another account (such as a savings account), and then move money from the savings account to the checking account only when you need to write a check. You can move the money from one account to another electronically or by going to your bank. Managing your checking account this way requires extra organization, and you run the risk of accidentally writing a check when there are not enough funds (money) in the checking account. Not having enough funds to cover a check is known as "insufficient funds" or "bouncing a check" and can happen if you don't manage your money properly or don't balance your checkbook (which we will cover later).

What is a Check?

A check can be in the form of a legal paper or electronic document. The paper format usually comes in books of 25. It allows you to remove money from your checking account and give it to another person or company. The recipient can deposit the check (money) directly into his or her own bank account or go to the bank and receive cash. When the recipient receives the money from the check, either in cash or by depositing it into his own bank account, this called "cashing a check".

How do you write a check, you ask? For this explanation, I will describe a paper check, as pictured below. Electronic checks are completed by accessing the bank through the internet and are slightly different than a paper check but work in the same manner.

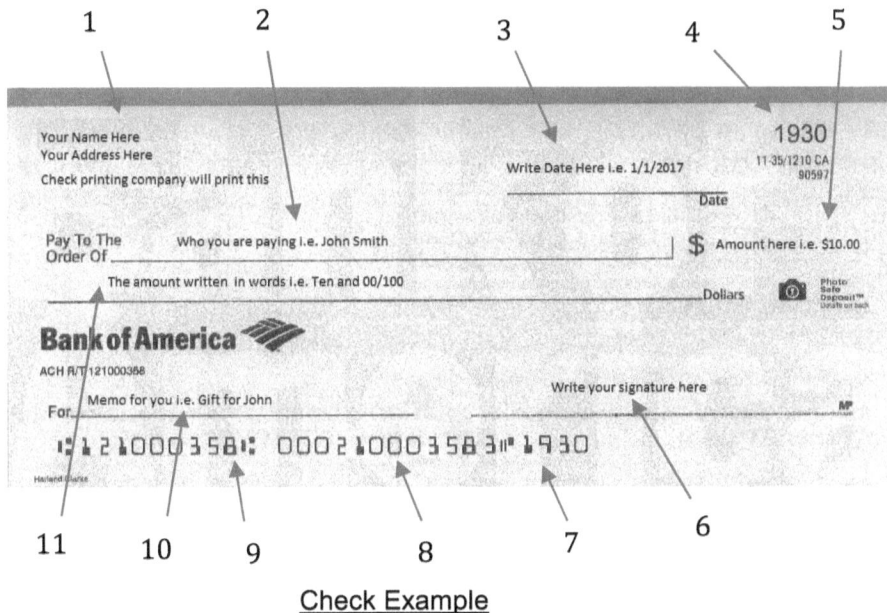

Check Example

1. Name and address of the account holder (you)
2. Pay To The Order Of: The name of the person or company who will receive the funds.
3. Date the check is written
4. The check number. Each check is numbered in numerical order.
5. Amount of check in dollars and cents, written in numerals. Example: For $10.50, write: 10.50
6. Your signature
7. The check number (the same as item number 4 above)
8. Your bank account number
9. The bank's "routing" number. This identifies the bank.
10. A place where you can write a note regarding the check; for example, what the check is for.
11. Amount of check in dollars and cents, written in words. Dollars are written in words. Cents are written as a fraction of a dollar.

Examples:
For $10.50, write: Ten and 50/100
For $150.37, write: One hundred fifty and 37/100

The blanks can be filled in by hand or printed with a typewriter (remember those things?) or computer. To prevent someone from making changes on your check, always use ink, never pencil. The check is signed by hand (unless you are a big corporation that uses a special stamp). Checks are usually ordered from the bank when you open the account. When you run low on checks, there is usually a form with the last check book which gives you instructions on ordering more checks, or you may reorder from the bank's website.

As electronic payments and online banking are becoming more and more common, checks are used much less often than in the past. Electronic payment methods such as Apple Pay, Pay Pal, Venmo, Zelle, and Bitcoin may eventually replace paper checks and credit cards.

Balancing Your Checkbook

Balancing your checkbook is something that everyone needs to know how to do, but often no one teaches you how to do it. To balance your checkbook means to keep track of how much money you have in your checking account, and then make sure that this amount agrees with the amount listed on your bank statement. That is, the amount that your records say are in the account and the amount that the bank says you have in the account must be equal, or "balance".

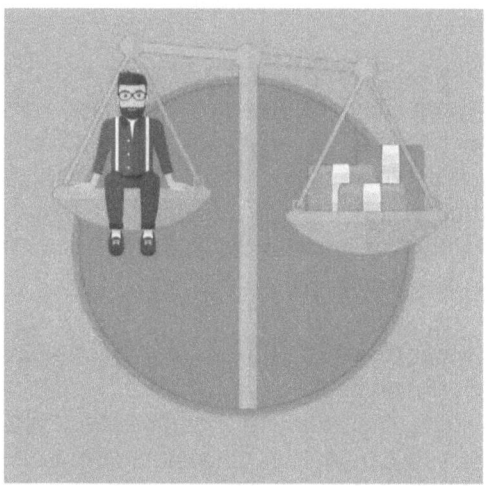

I initially learned how to balance my first checking account by reading the back of my statement and following the instructions. I remember that my mother never balanced her checkbook. She just tried to have enough extra money in the account to cover expenses, never knowing exactly how much money was in the account. I think this was because she was never taught how to balance her checkbook; hence, she never taught me.

Balancing your checking account is important because if you balance your checkbook, you can make a more accurate budget (which we will cover later).

Balancing will ensure that you always have enough money in your account to cover the checks you write. If there are insufficient funds in the checking account to cover the amount of the check, your check will "bounce", and the recipient will not receive their money. Your bank will charge you a fee for bouncing a check. There is a cost to process a bad check. A company who receives a bad check may charge you an additional fee, as well.

Banks offer a service called "overdraft protection". There is a fee for the service and there are conditions, but with overdraft protection the bank will cover up to a maximum dollar amount in case you write a check for more than what is in your account. Although there is a fee associated with this service, the recipient will receive the money, preventing other (more costly) fees and penalties, and you will avoid the embarrassment and trouble of a bounced check.

Your checkbook comes with a "register". This is a booklet where you keep a record of your checking account activity, so that you may balance your checkbook. The register has columns where you record the information, such as check number, date, recipient and/or description of the transaction, dollar amount of the transaction (check amount, deposit, fee, or withdrawal) and the balance. You can also create an electronic register, using a computer program such as Excel or QuickBooks. This will make your life a little easier because the software will do the calculations for you.

| 1 | 2 | 3 | 4 | 5 | 6 |

AD-Automatic Deposit • AP-Automatic Payment • ATM-Cash Withdrawal • MD-Mobile Deposit • DC-Debit Card • FT-Funds Transfer • SC-Service Charge • TD-Tax Deductible

NUMBER OR CODE	DATE	TRANSACTION DESCRIPTION	PAYMENT, FEE, WITHDRAWAL (-)		✓	DEPOSIT, CREDIT (+)		$	5000.00	
1817	7/18	First National Mortgage Bank	1850	00					3150	00
	7/19	Deposit - Paycheck				1225	00		4375	00
	7/22	Gas Company for June	57	25					4317	75
	7/24	Cash - ATM withdrawl	100	00					4217	75
	7/24	Visa Credit Card Payment for June	245	25					4072	50
	7/25	Interest for June				2	09		4074	59

Check Register Example

1. Check number
2. Date of check or transaction
3. Who the check is written to (the recipient), or a description of the transaction. In the example above, note that most of the transactions have no check number. This is because they were electronic transactions; a paper check was not used.
4. Amount of a check, fee, or withdrawal. This amount is subtracted from the balance.
5. Amount of a deposit or credit. This amount is added to the balance.
6. The amount of money remaining in the account (the balance). To obtain the balance:

Start with the initial account balance
Subtract all payments, fees, and withdrawals
Add all deposits and credits

It is important to record and keep track of all transactions. Be sure to include electronic transactions. It is equally important to compare your records with bank records, by checking your bank statement at least monthly. We all make mistakes! If you forget to record a check or withdrawal, it can result in a bounced check because you thought you had funds in the account to cover the check, when in fact you already spent the money but forgot to record it. Comparing your records with bank records will allow you to catch mistakes. And guess what?

Bank records may have errors, as well -- rare, but it can happen. Catch mistakes and/or control your budget before they become a problem.

Previously, balancing a checkbook was typically done right after you received your monthly statement from the bank. With electronic banking today, you may access your bank account online and balance your checkbook any time you choose. If you balance your checkbook using a paper statement, the longer you wait before balancing, the more complicated it will be, because you will have more transactions to add or subtract. The more often you balance your checkbook, the easier it is to do. With balancing online, the task is easier because the figures are more up to date.

When balancing your checkbook, you must take into consideration that some transactions may not yet appear on your bank statement. There are several reasons for this; here are just two examples:

- You wrote a check, but the recipient has not cashed it yet. In this case, the bank statement will show that you have more money in your account than your records show.
- You received a check and deposited it into your checking account. However, before the bank can release the funds to your account, it must verify that the check is good. This may take several days and causes a delay in the transaction. In this case, the bank statement will show that you have less money in your account than your records show.

In both cases, it is important to include the transactions in your balance, as it determines how much money you truly have to work with.

To balance your checkbook, have your checkbook register, bank statement, and a calculator in front of you. The bank statement can be in paper form (mailed to you by the bank) or on your computer screen if accessed online.

1. Determine the balance from your checkbook register (as described above):
    a. Start with the account balance you have in your register.
    b. Subtract all payments, fees, and withdrawals listed on your statement but not yet in your register (if any).
    c. Add all deposits and credits listed on your statement but not in yet in your register (if any).
    d. The resulting number is "Your" balance.
2. Obtain the "Bank" balance stated on the paper bank statement or by accessing your account online. We will refer to this as the "starting" Bank balance.

3. Compare all transactions on the bank statement or online transaction record to all transactions in your register. Remember that some transactions may not yet appear on
the bank statements.

    a.   Verify that the amount of each transaction matches.

    b.   For each transaction that appears correctly on both documents, mark it on your register (you can place a small "x" or check mark next to it). This will help later if you need to resolve a discrepancy (we'll talk about this below).

    c.   If a payment, fee, or withdrawal is missing from the bank statement, subtract that amount from the starting Bank balance.

    d.   If a deposit or credit is missing from the bank statement, add that amount to the Bank balance. But be careful here; if enough time has passed that the deposit or credit should have already appeared on the bank statement, contact the bank to resolve the issue. Don't rely on a deposit or credit amount until you know the funds are actually in the account.

    e.   If a transaction appears on the bank statement but not on your register, first verify that the transaction is correct. Did you forget to record the transaction? Is the transaction a bank error?

- If the transaction is correct, add it to your register and add or subtract the appropriate amount to Your balance.
- If the transaction is not correct (a bank error), contact the bank to resolve the error.

4. After you have determined that all transactions are accounted for, and all additions and subtractions are complete, compare Your balance to the Bank balance. Are they the same? Congratulations! You have just balanced your checking account! If not, follow the steps below to find out why.

What to do if Your Checking Account Does Not Balance

If Your balance and the Bank balance don't agree, you must find where the error occurs and resolve the issue. Here are some steps you can take to resolve the problem:

1. There may have been a simple error in adding or subtracting (calculations). Repeat your calculations to verify they were done correctly.

2. Check your register to see if you overlooked a check which was not cashed. This is where marking your register with an "x" (see step 3b above) comes in handy. If you find an entry that has no "x", you can quickly see if a check was not cashed, because it did not appear on the bank statement. You may want to make a note to yourself that the check is outstanding. This way, you will be reminded that this was an issue the next time you balance your checkbook.

Check the sequence of all your check numbers to make sure all are accounted for. Say you have check numbers 1102 and 1104 recorded, but number 1103 is missing, and you can't remember what the check was for. Note the difference in the Bank balance and Your balance and try to remember what that amount corresponds to. Maybe it's one of your monthly bills. For example, if you are off $145 and find that the electric bill last month was $145, this is probably your missing check. Some bank statements include images of checks which were cashed, which will solve your mystery as it will show who you paid and the amount.

Online banking makes balancing your checkbook easier since you can access your account via the internet at any time to see which deposits, expenses, fees, and checks have cleared. In addition, online information is more up to date than a paper statement delivered by mail.

If you have access to your account online, it is easy to look back into the past to see which checks have cleared or to compare the Bank amounts with Your amounts. If you have only paper statements, it is a good idea to keep the statements for several months so you can resolve any discrepancies later.

Balancing your checkbook is necessary so that you know how much money you have (or don't have!). Once you know this, you are on your way to creating a budget.

How Dan Disaster (Mis)Managed His Checking Account

Dan never balances his checkbook because he is busy, and he never took the time to learn how to do it. He never seems to have enough money to pay his bills. As a result of not balancing his checkbook and not accurately taking care of his finances, Dan bounced checks last month for his property tax payment and two of his credit card bills. The late fees on each of his credit cards was $45, for a total of $90. In addition, each credit card company charged a returned-check fee of $25, for a total of $50. Also, since the credit card companies did not receive payments, Dan will now pay more interest on the high credit card balances. Paying his property tax late was a bigger problem. The late fee was 10% of the payment due, $205. The cost for these three late payments, which occurred because Dan did not balance his checkbook and keep track of his checking account, cost him $345. This was wasted money that he could not afford to lose! For $345, he should have made time to learn how to balance his checkbook!

How Francine Frugal Correctly Manages Her Checking Account

Each month when Francine gets her bank statement, she carefully goes through all her payments and deposits. After balancing her checkbook and going over her outstanding bills for this month, she saw that she had $1,400 in her checking account but $1,700 in bills to pay. So, she went to her computer and transferred $500 from her savings account to her checking account; the electronic transfer was immediate. Francine then recorded the $500 transfer and updated the balance to $1,900 on her checking account register. She now has enough money in the account to cover her bills.

Francine then wrote a paper check for one of the bills and paid the other bills online, using the online bill-pay function her bank offers. Not only did she save time by not writing additional paper checks and mailing them, she also saved money by not paying for postage. After paying the $1,700 in bills, she recorded the transactions and calculated the new balance, and now has $200 remaining in the checking account. Her bills are paid on time, she has no late fees, and only the cost of one stamp to mail the paper check. Good job, Francine!

CHAPTER 4
CREDIT & DEBIT CARDS

Credit Cards: The "Money Pit" for most people - Money goes in but is never enough!

Don't have the cash you need right now? Just have to have that latest new electronic gadget? No problem! Charge it! Pay now, worry about it later! You have to pay only the monthly minimum payment, which may be as low as $15 a month. You can afford that, right? Or, can you?

Using a credit card is just like getting a loan from the bank. The amount you charge to the credit card is the amount of the loan; this is called the "principal". The bank will charge you for the loan, usually a percentage of the principal; this is called "interest". If you pay off the total amount of your loan (the principal) each month on time, you don't have to pay interest. If you pay only part of the principal, this means you will pay interest on the remaining principal.

Simple and Compound Interest Rates

There are two kinds of interest rates, simple and compound.

Simple interest is usually used for automobile loans or short-term loans and is calculated by multiplying the principal by the daily interest rate by the number of days between payments:

Principal x Daily interest rate x Number of days between payments

With a simple-interest-rate loan, each monthly payment first pays the interest for that month, and then the remainder goes towards the principal. This means the interest for each month is paid in full.

On the other hand, with a loan which has compound interest, each month some of the interest is added to the loan. This means a little is added to the principal each month, and the interest rate now applies to the new, larger, principal. Another way to look at it is that you pay interest on the interest! The longer you take to pay off the credit card, the more you will pay in interest. Earning compound interest is a good thing for savings accounts and investments but paying compound interest can cost more when you borrow money.

Alas, many credit cards don't use simple interest; they use compound interest instead. The calculations are complicated, but what you need to know is that compound interest on credit cards adds to your debt when you carry a balance (that is, when you don't pay off the entire balance each month). Interest is charged on a daily basis. High credit card interest rates and daily compounding can make paying off credit card debt very difficult.

Let's say you charge $2,000 to your credit card (the principal), and the bank requires a minimum monthly payment of $25. The credit card has an annual percentage rate (APR) of 20%, which is approximately $400 per year (less because your minimum payments reduces the actual amount of interest by paying off a small amount of the principle each month). If you pay the minimum monthly payment each month, then guess what? Since the credit card uses compound interest, you will incur more interest each day that you maintain the loan, which adds to the amount you owe. As the years go by, your balance will drop little by little, and you will eventually pay off the principal, but it will take more than ten years. In the end you will pay around $4,000. That's $2,000 you will pay in interest! To make matters worse, it is likely that you will use the credit card to make additional purchases, putting yourself more and more in debt each month.

Due to regulations, you will notice a little bit of information on your credit card statement. It will read something like, "If you make no additional charges to this card and each month you pay the minimum payment, the balance will be paid in 12.3 years."! Many people don't understand annual percentage rates or compounded interest. Remember, a credit card is really just a convenient loan with a VERY high interest rate. (If it was any higher, it could be considered "loan sharking", which is illegal. Take it from an old mobster movie. When someone did not pay back gambling debts, he got his legs broken! He didn't get cement shoes and thrown into the lake, because dead people can't pay back their loans!)

The lesson here is to use credit cards only as a convenience or in case of emergency. If you don't pay off a credit card in full each month, interest is charged on a daily basis; however, if you pay the principal in full each month within the allotted grace period, then interest is not charged.

Credit Card Terminology:

More terminology to know (must learn the language of the beast if you want to slay the beast!):

1. Credit Limit
    The maximum amount of money a bank or credit card will allow you to borrow/charge. Example: If I have credit card with a $3,000 credit limit, I may borrow/charge up to $3,000 with that card. If I use the card to purchase items for $2,000, I will have $1,000 remaining on my credit limit. If I make a $500 payment, then I will have $1,500 remaining on my credit limit. Credit card companies are quick to increase your credit limit because if you borrow more money, the bank will make more money. An increased credit limit makes it easier to make large purchases, which

in turn will increase the credit card balance and interest. If you pay only the minimum monthly payment, the debt will stretch out to more payments for years. This is how the bank ends up owning you.

2. Credit Card Balance
The amount of money you currently owe.

3. Minimum Monthly Payment
The minimum amount of money you must pay each month. The bank or credit card company determines this amount, and it will be stated on your credit card statement. The greater the balance, the higher the minimum payment.

4. Due date
The date the minimum payment is due. This will also be stated on your credit card statement.

5. Late date
Some bank or credit card companies will allow a grace period if you don't make the minimum payment by the due date. The late date is the date at which the grace period ends. If you do not pay by this date, you will be charged an additional fee (a late fee).

6. APR
Annual percentage rate. This is the amount a bank or credit card company will charge you each year for borrowing money and is a percentage of the amount owed (the principal or balance). At this writing, a credit card APR is usually between 18% and 26% annually. For instance, if the APR is 20%, then every year you will pay 20% of your balance in interest every year. APR is important to understand because the interest rate is so high. For example, say the interest rate for a home loan is 4% annually. Compare that to a credit card APR of 20%, and you can see this is a BAD deal! Legal loan sharking! (Yet, if you put your money in a savings account at the bank, they will pay you a whole1% interest, if you are lucky.)

7. Cash Advance
A service provided by most credit card companies, which allows you to use your credit card to withdrawal cash from an ATM or bank. Some credit card companies also have a special check that can be used this purpose, which can be deposited or cashed at a bank. These checks are usually mailed to you on a regular basis in a separate mailer or is included with your monthly paper statement. Stay away from these! In most cases, there a limit to the amount of cash you may withdrawal.

A cash advance is actually an expensive loan and should be used only in extreme emergencies. The credit card company will sometimes offer special temporary incentives, such as a low 4% interest rate for 90 days. But guess what happens after 90 days? The interest rate increases to the normal credit card APR of 18% to 26%. In addition to the interest, a cash advance can have other fees, such as a cash-advance fee (charged by the credit card company) and ATM or bank fees.

Credit card companies love for you to use this service. Just get some cash, and the amount will post to your credit card balance, plus any applicable fees. Getting into trouble and unable to pay the monthly payment minimum payment on one credit card? No problem, you can use a cash advance from one credit card company to pay off the other card. How convenient! Now the first card has a zero balance and you can use it to charge a whole bunch more! Problem solved, right? Wrong! You just created more debt, and you will have an extremely difficult time paying it off. Credit cards basically make it convenient to get a loan at a very high interest rate. Interest rates this high should be illegal, but banks get away with it!

Credit Card Management

The best way to utilize credit cards is to use them only for convenience when making purchases or payments, and then pay off the entire balance each month. If you pay the entire balance by the due date, then interest is not charged. By doing this, you essentially get a free loan from the credit card company each month. In addition, some credit card companies offer rebates based on a percentage of the amount you spend, usually around 1%-2%. In this case, you actually save money in the form of a rebate!

If you can't afford to pay off your credit card balance in full each month, it is best not to use the card. Be aware of the due date on your monthly statement. Avoid late payments, which can be $25 to $45 or more. Also, remember compound interest? If you make a payment late, you will pay additional interest, because the next billing cycle will include interest on the current balance, plus interest on any new charges. The charges keep adding up.

Don't worry that the credit card company won't make any money if you pay your credit card balance in full each month. They still make money because merchants pay a fee to accept credit card payments, usually 2%-4% of the total transaction amount.

What to Do If You Already Have Too Much Credit Card Debt

Do you have a mountain of credit card debt? Your priority must be to pay off the balances on your credit cards as fast as possible. Consider cutting up your credit cards and get a debit card instead. Cut out all non-mandatory spending. No new car, clothes, or electronics. No luxury items. No splurging on fancy restaurants. No "toys", jewelry, or expensive gifts. Pay only for food, utilities, mortgage, insurances, and any other mandatory expenses. If possible, even consider giving up any electronic device that you absolutely don't need for a while.

You must create a budget and a plan to pay off your credit card debt; otherwise, you will be a slave to the credit card companies until the debt is paid. See later chapters on "Creating a Budget" and "Getting Out of Debt", and you will be on your way to paying off your debt and gaining your financial freedom.

What Is A Debit Card?

A debit card looks like a credit card but is associated with one of your bank accounts. It is often a Visa or Master Card and is accepted any place that accepts credit cards. The difference is that it is not used to borrow money like you do with a credit card. When you use a debit card, the money is taken from your bank account. Therefore, you must already have funds in the account when you use the card to make a purchase. Your "credit limit" is the amount of money you put into your account.

Credit cards and debit cards both offer the convenience of not having to carry cash; however, the advantage of using a debit card is that you avoid the debt. On the other hand, because a debit card uses your own money, and a credit card uses the credit card company's money, credit card companies and banks usually offer better fraud protection services for credit card transactions than they do for debit card transactions. When you use a debit card, you need to enter your personal identification number (PIN) code to complete the transaction.

Credit Card Tale of The Uninformed

I have a friend (I'll call him Uninformed Bob), who is in his 20s and married. He and his wife want to buy a house. They have a problem that many young people have: They are unable to save enough money for the down payment. Uniformed Bob came up with the idea of putting part of the down payment on a credit card. Apparently, the credit card company was offering a great low interest rate for the first year, and he figured it was a great way to get an easy loan, without thinking of the ramifications. Short sighted and being uninformed was Bob's problem. He is a smart guy but lacked information and experience. I cringed when I heard this but did not say anything; I just let him finish the story. The story ended with him saying he was appalled that the real estate agent and the bank did not accept his credit card for the down payment. Lucky for him they didn't! He did not know why it was a bad idea, but the bank sure did.

What would have happened if they accepted his credit card? Bob and his wife would have purchased the house with two loans, a credit card loan to help with the down payment and a home loan (mortgage) for the remainder of the purchase price. The mortgage interest rate was less than 5%. The interest rate for first few months of the credit card loan was low, but after the "special rate" period expired, it would have increased to 25%. In addition to the monthly mortgage payment, they would have had a high credit card payment, which would have cost them thousands of dollars in interest over the life of the loan. At worst, the payments could have been unaffordable, and Bob and his wife could have ended up losing their home. If they lost the house, they would still have to pay off the credit card loan.

At the time, I had just started to write this book. Bob's situation motivated me to continue, as I have other friends like Bob who really need it! I am sure you do, too, so please share this book with them!

How Danielle Disaster (Mis)Manages Her Credit Cards

Danielle loves credit cards, so she has three of them. No purchase is out of reach. It doesn't matter that payday is not until next week when Danielle has a credit card with available credit left on it.

Danielle receives credit card applications almost every week in the mail, and each company has a great offer. When Danielle hit her credit limit on the first card, she applied for a new card at a different bank, and the new card offered twice the credit limit of the first card. Danielle figures this bank is better because the bank gave her a larger credit limit.

It did not take Danielle long to "max" out the credit limit on the second card. Then, she found the perfect solution. A third bank sent her a credit card application which she immediately sent in. Her first statement included a blank cash-advance check, with an offer to move the balance of her other credit cards to the new credit card, at a low 10% interest rate. Heck, this will save Danielle a lot of money because she currently pays 22% interest on the existing cards! So, Danielle used the cash-advance checks to pay off the balances on her first two credit cards. Yippee! Now her first and second cards were free to use again, and Danielle immediately started to use them (and she now has three credit card payments). Unfortunately, Danielle did not read the fine print regarding the new credit card and cash advance, which stated that the special 10% interest rate was only for six months. After six months, the interest rate would increase to 26%, which is even higher than her previous interest rates! She did not notice this until the monthly minimum payment on the new credit card increased. Now with three credit card payments, Danielle can barely afford the minimum payments. She just noticed the little box on one credit card statement that tells her if she pays the minimum payment, she will pay off the balance in 17 years! Danielle figures she will get a better job in the future and will pay off those cards in no time.

How Frank Frugal Correctly Manages His Credit Cards

Frank never buys anything on his credit card unless he knows he can pay the balance in full each month. He knows whether or not he can afford to make purchases, even large ones, because he created a budget and knows exactly how much money he can afford to spend each month. Last month, Frank used his credit card to purchase a new computer for $1,200. This month, when the charge appeared on his credit card bill, he accessed his bank account online and "wrote" an electronic check to the credit card company to pay the credit card balance in full. The bank's electronic functions allow Frank to choose the date on which the check will be released, so he scheduled the check to be sent one week before the due date. This guarantees that the bill will be paid within 24 hours of the scheduled date, so he is confident that the bill will be paid on time. Since Frank pays his credit card bills in full each month, and never carries a balance from month to month, he was not charged any interest or fees. (Also, some credit card companies charge an annual fee, but Frank made sure to choose a credit card which does not have an annual fee.) Frank bought his computer by using his credit card to borrow money for less than one month, with no fees. It was a free loan. Frank knows that if he was to pay only the minimum monthly payment, his $1,200 computer would end up costing him $2,000 or more. In addition, when Frank applied for his credit card, he made sure to choose one which earns points, so his $1,200 charge generated points which could be used to discount future purchases.

All too often people live paycheck to paycheck and are unable to save money. They have nothing left at the end of the month and get deeper into debt, often from credit cards.

Take-Away Lesson: Credit cards charge a very high interest rate. A sure path to financial ruin is to carry high credit card balances. It's a sure way to get yourself deeper in debt. It is super easy to fall into the pit of credit card debt and extremely difficult to climb out. The goal is not to carry a balance on a credit card. If you can't pay what you charge each month, don't charge it!

CHAPTER 5
LOANS

Loan Basics

The financial downfall for most people is getting into debt. Debt is money which is borrowed and then must be paid back. The amount paid back is usually more than the amount borrowed, due to costs associated with the loan, such as interest or fees. The money you borrow is a loan. Almost everyone will get a loan of some sort sooner or later. Large loans are used to purchase items such as a home or a car. Using a credit card is a way of obtaining a loan, a loan which has a very high interest rate, terms and fees.

This stuff is boring, but it's important to learn the terminology, as it will help you to understand the debt beast you are learning to tame.

Loan Terminology

Let's cover some basic loan terminology:

1. Mortgage:
    A loan to purchase property, such as a house or condominium.

2. Balance
    The amount of money owed on the loan.

3. Principal
    The amount owed on a loan.

4. Interest

The amount of money a bank or lender charges for the loan, a percentage of the principle amount.

5. Interest rate
    The percentage of the principle that the lender charges for the loan. Interest rates are typically based on a yearly (annual) timeline, known as the annual percentage rate (APR).

6. Fixed rate
    An interest rate which remains the same throughout the life of the loan.

7. Adjustable rate
    An interest rate that varies (it can increase or decrease) throughout the life of the loan. The terms are in the loan agreement, which you sign when obtaining the loan.

8. Minimum monthly payment
    The minimum amount of money you must pay to the lender each month.

9. Late fee
    A fee which is charged by the lender if you do not pay the minimum monthly payment by the due date, or by the grace period allowed by the lender.

10. Due date
    The date that the minimum monthly payment is due.

11. Late payment date
    The date which a late fee will be charge if the minimum monthly payment is not received on time.

12. Default
    Failure to repay the loan. Defaulting on a loan will result in consequences, such as repossession of your house or car, or having a collection agency come after you.

13. Down payment
    An initial payment which is made to the lender, prior to obtaining a loan. The down payment is part of the cost of the item which is purchased. For example, say you obtain a loan for a house which costs $100,000, and the lender requires a 20% down payment. You would give the lender an initial payment of $20,000, and the loan would be for the remaining $80,000.

14. PMI

    Private Mortgage Insurance. This is insurance which you must purchase if the down payment on your home loan is less than a specified amount (often, less than 20% of the purchase price). It protects the lender against loss if the borrower defaults on the loan.

15. Statement

    A document which has details regarding your loan account, including balance, minimum amount due, due date, late date, payments, interest, and so on. Statements can be on paper or electronic and are usually generated each month.

16. Payment Coupons

    A book with 12 coupons, one for each month in the year. Typically given to the homeowner each year from the mortgage lender. On the coupon is the payment amount needed to be submitted the due date, and the address where the payment needs to be sent.

I know it all sounds like Greek now, but it will make sense after the following chapters, when we put these words into real life situations.

CHAPTER 6
HOME LOANS

If someone would have told me when I was young, how much money I would have to make in order to buy a house in the neighborhood where I grew up, I would have studied much harder in school! As I mentioned before, I worked for a wealthy businessman throughout college. My boss Phil told me, "Rod, the way to get ahead and make money in your life is to own your own business. The way to make and save enough money for your own business is to get a good education. A good education will allow you to earn good money, so that you can AFFORD to save enough to start your own business." He then asked me for a nickel. He said he asked for the nickel because people will listen when they pay for advice but not when they get advice for free! I paid him the nickel and have never forgotten this lesson.

<u>My Home Story</u>

I live in Southern California. The cost to purchase a home here is outrageous. We live in a small house, less than 1000 square feet, in a middle-class neighborhood, which was assessed this year at over $600,000. For a young couple to buy a small home like the one I live in, they would need to get a home loan and come up with the 20% down payment. Can they afford this? In 2008, there was a disastrous housing market bubble and stock-market crash. A significant contributing factor was that many lenders made loans to people who not afford them, but we will talk about that later.

Where housing costs are high, such as in Southern California, coming up with the down payment for a house is one of the biggest obstacles people face. For our $600,000 house, a 20% down payment is $120,000! Who these days has an extra $120,000 cash laying around? Our son lives in San Francisco and really wants to buy a house there. The average cost of a very small home in San Francisco is even higher, more than $1,000,000 for a home that needs work!

My first wife and I purchased our first home in 1987 for $160,000. At that time, we could not afford a 20% down payment ($32,000) or even a 10% down payment ($16,000). We had only $6,000 saved and a baby on the way! To come up with a 10% down payment, we borrowed $10,000 from a wealthy uncle. A 10% down payment meant also that we had to purchase PMI, which was added to the loan amount and increased the monthly payments. Back then, the interest rate was around 13%, and I often wondered if we could afford the payments because I made only $10 per hour at the time, not much when your mortgage payment is close to $1,400 per month. Fortunately, my wife worked, as well. I could not have done it on my own, and we would not have qualified for the loan with only one income. Nowadays, partners must often both work so that they can afford to buy a home. The days of "Ozzie and Harriet", "Leave It To Beaver", and "Father Knows Best", where the husband comes home from work to the housewife who has been cleaning and cooking all day are long gone!

I saw an interview with a member of the wealthy Rockefeller family. He said that the women's liberation movement in the 1960's was funded by world bankers and organized by his father. In the traditional household of the 1950's, the father went to work and the mother stayed home with the kids. The bankers figured out that if women joined the workforce, households would have more money. In turn, the government would benefit from increased taxable income, and banks and lenders would benefit from increased business.

Whew, I digress, now back to home loans…

So, to make things simple for our real-life lesson, let's say you want to purchase a house in a small, rural, Midwest town, for $125,000. A 20% down payment means you need to come up with $25,000. The lender is offering a fixed interest rate of 5%. This means every year you will pay an extra 5% of the amount of money you owe, as a cost for borrowing the money. Since you will make a $25,000 down payment, your loan will be for $100,000. The first year, you will pay approximately $5,000 in interest (5% of $100,000). The most common home loan a 30-year loan, which means it will be paid in full in 30 years (a 30-year pay-off time). Other pay-off times are available, such as 20 or 15 years. A 30-year loan will have lower monthly payments over a longer time period. A 20-year or 15-year loan is paid off in a shorter time but will have higher monthly payments.

Let's look at the specifics of a $100,000 loan with a 5% annual fixed interest rate (APR) for 30 years:
Total amount of loan: $100,000
Monthly payment: $537

Doesn't sound too bad right? Now, let's look at how much interest we will pay over 30 years:
Total amount of interest over 30 years: $93,320
Total amount paid to lender: $193,320

Now let's look at what happens if we cut the loan time to 15 years:
The monthly payment goes up to $791.
Total amount of interest over 15 years: $42,380
Total amount paid to lender: $142,380

The difference between a 15-year loan and a 30-year loan is a savings of $50,940 over the life of the loan! With a 15-year loan, you will pay less than half of the interest of a 30-year loan, yet payments increase by only $254 per month.

So, this means that if you can afford the 15-year loan, you can save a boatload of money! Think of what you could do with that extra $50,000 dollars! If you want to purchase a home in Southern California, multiply these figures by at least four times, due to the higher cost of real estate. Then you will see really big numbers. Does saving almost $200,000 appeal to you Southern Californians?

Pre-Payment Penalty

A pre-payment penalty is a fee the lender will charge if you pay off your loan early. For example, say you take out a -30-year loan and then pay a little extra each month so that the loan is paid off in less than 30 years. You will save money by paying less interest; however, if the terms of your loan include a pre-payment penalty (a fee), you will pay the penalty fee. Lenders know that they will make less money in interest if you pay off your loan early, so some add this pre-payment penalty into the loan contract. As if they aren't already making a load of money off you! So, read your loan contract and make sure there is no pre-payment penalty clause. If there is, have the lender remove it. If the lender won't remove it, find another lender.

Reducing the Principal

What if you can currently afford a 15-year loan but fear that circumstances may change to where you would be better off with a 30-year loan and a lower monthly payment? Go with the 30-year loan. When paying off a loan, you have the option to pay extra to reduce the amount owed. This gives you flexibility because you can still make higher payments when your financial situation allows but lower your payments to the amount agreed to on the loan if your financial situation should change.

There are several ways to pay extra to reduce the amount owed. One way is to arrange with the lender to pay one-half of the monthly payment every two weeks. Monthly payments come to 12 payments per year. Paying one-half the monthly amount every two weeks will result 12.5 payments, an extra one-half payment each year. It's not a lot, but it will reduce the time it takes to pay off the loan, and therefore, reduce the amount of interest paid.

Another way is that when you make your regular payment, to pay a little extra each time. It is important when using this method to make sure the extra funds go towards paying the PRINICPAL only (not to pay any interest). You can check with your lender to see how to accomplish this. This method reduces the principal faster and also decreases the amount of interest paid over the life of the loan.

A third way is to pay an extra lump sum whenever possible. That is, when your financial situation allows, you work with the lender to make an extra payment in any amount. Again, make sure the extra payment goes towards the PRINCIPAL only.

Using one of these options may be good if your employment or future financial situation is uncertain. Again, make sure there is no prepayment penalty if you decide to pay off a loan earlier than expected.

CHAPTER 7
HOUSING DECISIONS: RENT OR BUY?

Should you purchase or rent a home? Many people choose to rent houses or apartments for a variety of reasons. For some, rent makes sense if employment dictates that they will move from place to place. Some rent because they don't want the responsibilities of home ownership. Others want to purchase a home but rent because they are unable to save enough money for the down payment. Remember my small house in Southern California which is worth $600,000? For a 20% down payment, you would have to come up with $120,000 cash and qualify for a loan of $480,000, which is totally out of reach for most people. For others, it is attainable, but only through careful budgeting and discipline. In addition, with a 5% interest rate, payments on a 30-year loan amount of $480,000 will be more than $2,500 per month, or more than $3,800 per month with a 15-year loan.

If you rent, that money is gone forever. If you purchase, you pay a lot of money in interest to the bank, but you also pay the principal, which means that eventually the house will be yours (if you make all the payments).

When you obtain a home loan, it is really the lender who owns most of the home. As you pay down the principal, you own a greater percentage of the home, and the lender owns less. Your home equity is the amount you would receive if you sold your home, after all debts on the home are paid, including the remaining money owed on the mortgage. As you pay off more of the principal, your equity increases. It is like paying into a savings account every month, but instead of dollars, you own an increasing percentage of your property with dollar value. If the value of the house goes up, so does the dollar amount of your equity (real estate can be a good investment if property values go up!).

In addition, if you buy a place to live, the money you pay in interest each year is tax deductible. For example, if in one year you earned $50,000 and paid $15,000 in interest on your home loan, you would pay income tax on the difference, which is $35,000. This is called the "mortgage interest tax deduction". It is one of the sacred cows of our complex tax system and is unlikely to be altered any time soon. If you pay rent, your payments are not tax deductible unless you have a home-based business. If you own your home AND you have a home-based business, you get the mortgage interest deduction AND may be able to deduct some of your home expenses (restrictions apply).

Pros and Cons of Renting

Pros of Renting:
- Flexibility of moving when you want
- No big down payment needed
- Payment may be lower than a house payment
- Smaller space - lower expenses, utilities
- Easier to keep clean
- No yard to maintain if you are in an apartment
- No maintenance to worry about if you are in an apartment

Cons of Renting:
- You don't build equity (property ownership)
- The money you spend for rent is gone forever
- Monthly payments (rent) may increase
- Less privacy
- Cannot make changes to the building or landscaping as you wish
- Can be noisy due to neighbors
- Parking may be limited
- Storage is limited
- Often requires a security deposit and the first and last month's rent before you can move in. The security deposit is returned if there is no damage when you move out.
- May require a background or credit check

Pros and Cons of Buying

Pros of Buying:
- Build equity (you will eventually own the property once your loan is paid)
- Monthly payments will not increase (with a fixed-rate loan)
- You own the property and can change the building and landscaping as you wish (unless you have a homeowner's association (HOA) with restrictions)

- o   Color of interior and exterior
- o   Floor plan
- o   Yard and landscape as you like
- o   Appliances, flooring, furnishings
- You can usually choose your cable company, internet service provider, or satellite dish company.

Cons of Buying:
- Large down payment needed
- Need an income which meets loan qualifications
- Moving is not easy, as you may have to sell your house
- Not good if you move frequently (e.g., due to job demands)
- If you can't keep up with the payments, you can lose your house, including your down payment and any equity
- You are responsible for upkeep and maintenance, such as:
  - o   Plumbing - leaks and sewage clogs
  - o   Electrical problems
  - o   Heating and air conditioning problems
  - o   Painting inside and out
  - o   Roof - fixing leaks, replacing old roofs
  - o   Mowing the lawn, pulling weeds
  - o   Trimming the trees and bushes, other landscaping
- Utilities are often more expensive, including water, power, and rubbish removal
- Homeowner insurance is required if you have a mortgage
- Property taxes (usually 1%+ of the total property value, paid annually)
- You are stuck with whatever neighbors you have, good AND bad.

House or Condominium? Pros and Cons

Okay, so you have decided to buy instead of rent. Should you buy a condominium (condo), townhouse, or house? A condo is similar to an apartment; it is housed in one (or several) building which contains multiple units. A townhome is a single-family home which shares at least one wall with another townhome and usually has a garage. A house is a separate building; it does not usually share walls with another unit or home.

Often with condos and townhouses, you own the building or unit but not the land. Instead, you may have a long-term lease agreement on the property. A 99-year lease is not uncommon. Different options have pros and cons. Condos almost always have "association fees", fees which are used to pay for maintenance on common areas, such as swimming pools or landscaping. Let's take a look at the some of the pros and cons of each.

<u>Pros of Owning a House (Versus a Condo or Townhome) *:</u>

- You own the land and the building. This means you are in charge and no one can tell you what you can or cannot do on your land, within reason. You will still need to pull permits if you wish to do building construction, and any major changes to things like electrical and gas but you have more control.
- The land and house both have value. Land ownerships means that even if the house is lost, for example by fire or natural disaster, the land still has value.
- You may paint your house whatever color you like. You may also do anything you like with the landscaping so long as you are in compliance with local regulations.
- You usually may add on to the house (with the proper permits) and put any kind of roof or siding you desire.
- You may choose your cable or satellite company or mount a satellite dish on your home.

- Privacy. A single-family house usually does not share walls or ceilings with another dwelling, allowing more privacy for the owner.
- Private outdoor and garage space. A house generally has at least some private yard space and a private garage or storage space.
- A house may gain a greater percentage of value versus a condominium over the same length of time.

*There are exceptions to these "pros" of owning a house, as there are some housing developments which do have rules regarding what you may and may not do with your home. There may also be association fees. A "gated" community is an example of this where the entire development is surrounded by walls with access through one or more security gates. There may also be shared swimming pools and recreation areas which are paid for by the association fees.

<u>Cons of Owning a House (Versus a Condo or Townhome)</u>

- You are responsible to maintain the structure and landscape. Gardening. Plumbing. Electrical. Roof leaks. Tree trimming. Lawn mowing. Need to rake leaves or remove snow? All of these are your responsibility. Do you have a swimming pool? It is your responsibility to make sure it is cleaned and maintained.

<u>Pros of Owning a Condo (Versus a House)</u>

- You don't have to worry about maintaining the landscape, as the homeowners' association will hire gardeners to maintain the grounds. Each unit usually does not have its own front or back yard; instead, yards are usually part of the common areas. Common areas are areas which are used by all the residents of a condominium complex, such as yards, pools, gyms, and recreation rooms.

- Snow removal and pool maintenance is often included in your monthly association fees.
- Typically, the living space is smaller and easier to maintain, and utilities are less costly, depending on size.

Cons of Owning a Condo (Versus a House)

- You will pay a monthly homeowners' association fee, which can range from a few hundred to more than a thousand dollars a month. Fees often increase over time.
- You don't get to choose what the exterior of the building looks like, such as color, roofing or siding materials, or other items. Usually, all the units of a condominium complex look alike; there is no individuality.
- You often may not install anything that might be considered an eyesore, such as a satellite dish or TV or radio antenna, without approval of the association.
- Homeowners are often responsible for additional capital expenditures, such as a new roof or repaving the parking lot. You will have to pay even if you don't want the improvement or if you think the work does not need to be done. If the association and a majority of homeowners agree that the work needs to be done, you will be assessed the additional fees. I owned a condominium in Mammoth Lakes, California. When the association decided to put a new roof and new siding on the condo complex, each unit was assessed at $8,000 to complete the work. Some condo owners were retired and on fixed incomes. There were a few who had to sell their condos because they were unable to pay the $8,000.
- Less privacy. Condos share walls (and often, ceilings) with each other. Neighbors are very close together.
- Less space. If you want your own yard, garage, or outdoor space, a condo is not for you.
- Since most condos do not have a yard, if you want to plant flowers or have a vegetable garden, you may not be able to. Many condos do have a small patio or balcony area with room for potted plants.

Hidden Expenses of Home Ownership

Here are some expenses that you will have to pay if you own your home. These expenses are in ADDITION to your mortgage.

1. Property tax:
    Generally 1 to 1.25% of the total assessed value of your home, which you must pay every year. For example, if the house is appraised at $500,000, and the property tax is 1%, you will pay $5,000 per year. In California, the property tax is split into two payments, due in November and February. (The February payment may be made as late as April without penalty; however, April is a terrible deadline date since income taxes are due also in April. If you owe income taxes, you could be hit with two very large bills in the same month.)

2. Homeowner's Insurance:
    This is insurance to cover loss in case of fire or other damage, theft, or liability if someone is hurt on your property. Coverage varies, depending on the policy, as does the cost. On our small house, the homeowner's insurance is around $1,100 per year. Insurance costs will be higher if you are in an area which has higher risks for such things as fire, floods, or earthquakes. In California, earthquake insurance is not included in the regular homeowner's policy; instead, it may be purchased as an optional policy with a high deductible. The deductible is an amount of money you must first pay out of pocket before the insurance company will pay for loss or repairs. For example, if you have a $100,000-dollar repair bill and a $30,000 deductible (high deductibles are common with earthquake insurance), you pay the $30,000, and the insurance company will pay the remaining $70,000. The deductible amount is part of the insurance "contract" and can be as low as a few hundred dollars or as high as thousands of dollars. Lenders require you to have homeowner's insurance as a condition of your home loan, because they own most or part of your home until the loan is paid. Once you pay off

your loan, having insurance is not mandatory, but it would be foolish not to have it. A fire could leave you homeless if you don't have insurance to cover the loss.

3. Utilities:

The costs of natural gas, electricity, water, telephone, garbage removal and/or other items needed to run your home. These costs can be highly variable, depending on where you live. If you live where it is hot and air-conditioning is used, your monthly electric bill can be $100 to $1000 per month or more, depending on the size of the house, how hot it gets in your area, and utility rates. If you live where it is cold, it could cost hundreds or thousands of dollars to heat your home. We have friends who live in Alaska. One friend owns a very large house and has an annual cost of around $8,000 for heating oil each winter.

A multi-year drought in Southern California caused water costs to skyrocket so much that people let their lawns die; some removed their lawns altogether and planted drought-tolerant landscapes.

How The Disaster Family Found Their Dream Home...And Lost It!

Dan and Danielle Disaster have it all. They are not wealthy, but Dan drives his sports car, and Danielle drives her new BMW. Dan also has a cool full-size 4x4 pickup truck. The truck cost $50,000, and the loan had a low 1.9% annual interest rate, so Dan couldn't pass up such a good deal. The Disasters currently rent a nice apartment and pay $2,500 a month. They really want to own their own home because they want to buy a boat and a recreational vehicle (RV) and need a place to park their new "toys".

Dan makes good money working in construction, and Danielle makes a little extra money working part time at the local college. Danielle recently inherited $160,000. This will allow the Disasters to make a down payment on a house selling for up to $800,000. They found their $800,000 dream home in a nice suburban neighborhood in Southern California.

As a result of their carefree spending, Dan and Danielle managed to rack up $15,000 in credit card debt. They have their monthly car payments, which increased to $1,800 per month when Dan bought the truck, which he needs to tow the boat he is planning to buy. Since the Disasters currently have a solid income, they qualified for a home loan even though they carry other debts. The Disasters chose an adjustable-rate, 30-year loan because monthly payments on the adjustable-rate loan were lower than the payments on a fixed-rate loan (Danger! An adjustable-rate loan means the rate – and payments – can increase over time!).

Fast-forward. The Disasters purchased the home and have been living there several years now. Things have been tight financially. Dan and Danielle did not realize their property taxes would be around $8,000 a year. They really had to scrape in order to come up with money. This year, their adjustable-rate mortgage payment went up, increasing the monthly payment by over $500.

To make matters worse, a slowdown in construction caused the company that Dan works for to see a great reduction in construction jobs and Dan was laid off (supposedly only until things get a little better in the construction industry). Dan is not qualified to do any other type of work. The construction slump is everywhere, and no one is hiring. After some months, the Disasters had not made any mortgage or car payments or paid any of their credit card bills. Danielle's job was only enough to cover the food bills and their cell phone bill which they felt they could not live without.

First, the credit card companies started called, saying they did not receive payments for the last three months. Then, the lenders who provided the car and truck loans came calling. After a few months, all three vehicles were repossessed. Dan and Danielle then received an eviction notice, along with a notice that the bank is foreclosing on the house. The house – Gone! The down payment, $160,000 -- Lost! The principal paid over the last several years –Gone! Dan and Danielle are homeless, without even a car to live in. Disaster for the Disasters!

Frank and Francine Frugal want to purchase a house and know their biggest difficulty is coming up with the down payment. They feel they are lucky because they live in the Midwest where homes are still affordable. After searching for homes in their area, Frank and Francine found that a small house which fits their needs would be about $150,000. They know they need a 20% down payment, which amounts to $30,000. Frank found a mortgage calculator online which enabled him to calculate the monthly payment for a $120,000 loan at the current 4% interest rate. He found that for a 30-year loan, the monthly payment would be only $573. Heck, the Frugals currently pay $800 per month to rent their apartment. What a deal! Checking further, Frank found that the monthly payment for a 15-year loan would be $888, not much more than their current rent. Frank figured out that even though monthly payments would be higher with a 15-year loan, the 15-year loan would save him and Francine thousands of dollars in interest payments over the life of the loan. Also, when obtaining a loan, they will make sure to get a fixed-rate loan so that their payments will always be the same, and not increase.

The Frugals both have steady jobs and a modest income. Together, Frank and Francine worked out a budget. They made a list of all their expenses and determined how much money they would spend each month. They also determined how much money they earned. When making the list of expenses, Frank and Francine estimated the costs of utilities and property taxes. They obtained estimates for homeowners' insurance. During Frank's research, he found that a rule of thumb is that a mortgage payment should not be more than one-third of the total household income. After projecting future expenses, Frank and Francine determined they could afford the monthly $888 payment if they did not buy that new car they had their eye on. Instead, they would buy a used car which they were more than happy to do if it allowed them to purchase a house.

The Frugals already have $20,000 saved up and need just $10,000 more for the down payment. In addition, they would like to save another $10,000 to have as a backup to cover any unforeseen costs. Frank and Francine created a budget and figure that if they really buckle down on spending and cut some unnecessary expenses, it will take them two years to save the additional $20,000.

Two years later, the Frugals achieved their goal. They had enough for the down payment plus $10,000 extra in savings. Of course, the house they had found the previous year was no longer available, but they purchased one they liked even better in the same price range. In addition, during the past two years, the interest rate actually went down, so their payments were even less than they had anticipated. They now had their own home with costs well within their means, enabling them to pay their bills without worry and stress. The Frugals continued to put money into their savings account each month, so that they would have available funds in case of any emergencies that may arise.

A few years after purchasing the home, Frank was laid off and was out of work for six months. Thankfully, because the Frugals had their savings and lived frugally, they were able to pay their bills during this time on Francine's income alone.

Delayed gratification and discipline enabled Frank and Francine to attain their goal of homeownership. Happy ending!

CHAPTER 8
"UNDERWATER MORTGAGE"

Usually, home values are expected to increase. However, there have been times when home values decrease. If this should happen, the market value of a home may become less than the loan principal. In other words, you may owe more on your mortgage than the home is worth. This debt is called an "underwater" mortgage.

A little history: For several years prior to 2008, housing prices reached a level where the average person could not afford to purchase a home or even save enough for a down payment. Lenders responded to this by creating different kinds of home loans which would make it easier for the average person to purchase a home. One example was a loan that required no down payment. Another example was a loan that had no interest for the first few years. These sounds great, right? Wrong! There was a catch! These types of loans sounded great at first, but the catch was that the loan terms changed over time, and these terms were good for the lender and terrible for the borrower.

These terrible loans were given to people who could not truly afford to own the home they selected. These people obtained the loans because the initial terms sounded great, but they did not understand how the later terms would affect them. For example, a loan with no down payment means that you don't need to have a large amount of money up front, but the principal is significantly higher, and therefore, the monthly payment and the amount of interest you will pay over the life of the loan is significantly higher. How about a loan which has no interest rate for the first few years? When those first few years have passed, you will then be charged an interest rate which is much higher than the interest rate on a traditional loan would have been.

How did these loans come into play with underwater mortgages? In 2008, there was a financial crisis, and it all came crashing down. During this time, home values dropped dramatically, causing many people to have underwater mortgages. Let's say you purchased a home for $500,000 and obtained one of those loans which required no down payment. Due to the financial crisis, the value of your home dropped to $400,000, but you still owe close to $500,000 on the mortgage. You are "underwater" by almost $100,000. Ouch!

The financial crisis also affected the job market. Many people lost their jobs and were unable to pay their mortgage. A homeowner in this situation couldn't even sell the home to pay off the loan because the home was worth less than the amount owed. Unable to pay their mortgages or sell their homes, homeowners across the nation walked away from their homes and went into foreclosure. Foreclosure is when the bank takes full ownership of the home and evicts the owner due to non-payment of the mortgage. People who had owned their homes for a short time lost relatively little, as they had paid little on the principal. People who had owned their homes for a longer time and had made more payments lost more. All of these people ruined their credit.

Lenders also had significant losses. They lost the amount which was still owed on the loans less any money they could recover from a foreclosure sale. In addition, lenders, who are not generally in the real estate business, now owned thousands of abandoned homes across the nation, many of which were neglected and in disrepair. The homes had to be repaired and sold or sold as-is in order to recoup their losses.

This was a part of what caused the "housing bubble" and stock market collapse of 2008. Another factor was that lenders gave "subprime" or "high-risk" loans, which are loans given to people who have a bad credit rating. In other words, these people had a history of not paying bills on time or defaulting (not paying back) on loans, (which is recorded and reported by credit reporting agencies). The situation was a disaster waiting to happen. Defaulting on a home loan will cause damage to your credit rating, which makes it more difficult for you to get a loan in the future.

I have a good friend who bought a beautiful craftsman style, two-story house in a very nice neighborhood in Southern California. It needed a bit of work, so he spent the money to fix it up and was able to sublet (rent out rooms) part of the house to help cover expenses. He got a great price on the house, and the value of the house appreciated considerably during the time he owned it. He had a good job, and this was the type of investment that would generate a nice nest egg for him for future real estate investments and/or business startups. It was the perfect house, in the perfect neighborhood, and he bought it at a good price.

Then...the 2008 market crash hit. The value of the house plummeted, and the house was "underwater" in a big way. He had to walk away from it. He did everything right. Few saw the housing bubble that exploded in 2008 coming. Bad luck!

CHAPTER 9
CREDIT RATINGS

Loaning money always carries a risk that the borrower may not pay back the loan. Before giving you a loan, lenders want to have an idea of that risk, so they will check to see if you have a good history with previous financial commitments. There are companies who obtain records of your previous financial commitments so that they can assess (and rate) the likelihood that you will pay back your loan. This is called a credit rating. Credit ratings are also used in other situations where a financial obligation is important, such as renting an apartment.

Credit ratings are given by companies such as Transunion, Experian, and Equifax. Credit card companies, banks, lenders, landlords, and others provide your payment history to these companies, which include data about on-time payments, late payments, and non-payments (defaults). If you make late payments, default on loans, or carry a high balance (lots of debt), the credit rating companies will know. A credit report shows every credit card you have ever owned, every loan you have ever had, balances, and payment history. Payment history is the biggest factor when determining your credit rating. Based on this information, lenders can better determine their risk when giving you a loan. A high credit rating means that you are a lower risk for default. A low credit rating means that you are a higher risk for default. In some cases, a high credit score will allow you to qualify for a lower interest rate because you are considered a low risk for default.

Credit rating scores range between 300 to 850. A score of 300 to 640 is considered bad, and you can usually obtain only a "secured" loan if you have a rating in this range. A secured loan means that you must have something to use as collateral, such as a car or a house; this is something of value that the bank can take from you if you default on your loan. A loan may also be secured by having a second party co-sign for your loan. In the event of non-payment, the person who co-signed the loan is liable for payment. A credit score of 640 to

680 is fair, meaning you may obtain a loan, but often only one with a higher interest rate. A credit score of 680 to 720 is good; you have a good chance of obtaining a loan, and with better interest rates. A score of 720 to 850 is considered the best; this qualifies you for the best interest rates and the best likelihood your loan will be approved.

If you want to check or raise your credit rating, the first step is to get a copy of your current credit report; this way you can see what you are up against. Each of the credit agencies will provide you with one free report per year.

Keep your credit in good standing. If needed, set calendar reminders a week or two before each bill is due to make sure bills are paid on time. Regular payments can also be scheduled to be paid automatically with most online bank accounts so that you will never be late. Repeated late payments can negatively affect your credit rating. This can be easily avoided with a little organization. In addition, you should make every effort to keep your credit balances as low as possible. On credit cards, pay the balance off in full each month.

CHAPTER 10
HOME EQUITY CREDIT LINES

Also known as a "second mortgage", a home equity credit line allows you to borrow money against the principal that you have in your home. For example, say you bought a house for $300,000 and put $60,000 down, so the original loan was for $240,000. Over the years you paid down the loan, so the balance owed is now $100,000. This means that you still owe $100,000, but you have $200,000 of equity in the house (providing it's still worth $300,000). A home equity line of credit allows you to borrow a percentage of your equity, at an interest rate which is usually higher than a home loan rate but much lower than other types of loans. A home equity loan has a much lower interest rate than a credit card by far.

In addition to a lower interest rate, another advantage to a home equity loan is that the interest you pay may be tax deductible at the end of the year. Say you earned $50,000 in a year and paid $10,000 in mortgage and home equity loan interest. You may deduct that $10,000 from your earnings, meaning you pay income taxes on $40,000 instead of $50,000. That's a big deal! Home equity loans may be used for major home improvement projects, such as adding a room or putting on a new roof. There are no restrictions as to what you may use the money for. Some people use it to pay off credit card debt, which is not such a bad idea. Since a home equity loan interest rate is much lower than a credit card interest rate, you can reduce the amount of interest you will pay.

But, be careful! There is a downside to a home equity loan; it is that this loan puts your home at risk. A home equity loan is similar to a mortgage loan, in that you may lose your home if you do not make the minimum payments. The bottom line is not to spend money you can't pay back. If you don't pay back a home mortgage loan or a home equity loan, you could end up losing the home!

CHAPTER 11
AUTOMOBILE PURCHASES AND LOANS

First of all, know that a car is generally a poor financial investment, because a car loses value the second you drive it off the car lot. Compare this to an investment in real estate or stock, which usually increases in value over time.

On the other hand, although purchasing a car is not usually a good financial investment, there are many reasons that owning a car may be a necessity. One reason is if the vehicle is used for business. Another reason is the lack of other available transportation. Remember the song lyrics "Walking in LA, nobody walks in LA"? It's not because Los Angeles residents don't like walking. It's because the city is very spread out and does not have a robust public transportation system. For most people in the Los Angeles area, using public transportation is not feasible, due to lack of availability, high cost, and increased travel time. Time and sanity are valuable! The ability to get to work and other places in less time is valuable!

Here is another reason to own a car. One thing that LA is famous for (besides Hollywood) is traffic! And long commutes! I know people who commute to work two hours one way. This means they are in their car four hours each day, spending a significant amount of their waking hours in Los Angeles traffic. I understand why it would be good to have a nice, comfortable ride, since they spend so much time in the car (just like it's important to have a good quality mattress, since you spend one-fourth to one-third of your life in bed!).

On a side note, here's a little tidbit to ponder. There is a conspiracy theory that back in the 1940's and 1950's, General Motors (GM) bought the Los Angeles streetcars and trolleys, only to shut them down to allow the auto industry to grow.

I don't know if this is true, but it is true that Los Angeles is the automobile mecca of the U.S., and GM did buy out the public transportation at that time.

So, we know a car is a poor financial investment but can be a good investment for other reasons. It may be a necessity to get to work. If you can't get to work, you may not be able to earn money. No money, no honey! However, owning a car does not mean you have to buy an expensive car. I think it is interesting that Leonardo DiCaprio, a wealthy Hollywood celebrity, can drive any car he wants, but he drives a Toyota Prius because it is clean, cheap, and efficient. It is also a political statement for him against global warming and shows his support of the "Green Movement". On the other hand, I know people who don't have much money but drive a Mercedes Benz, Cadillac, BMW, or Lexus, even though they can't afford to maintain their house and yard. Got to look good! To some people, status and appearance are more important than financial security. I have learned that some people can buy an expensive car if they save their money, but few can afford the higher maintenance costs associated with a luxury vehicle. Keep this in mind before you buy. A $20,000 economy car will get you places just as well as a $70,000 luxury car.

Just think about what would happen if you are 35 years old, and instead of spending that extra $50,000 to purchase the luxury car, you invested that money. Over the next 30 years until you retire, that $50,000 can grow to over $500,000. Compounding interest at work. You make money on your initial investment, and you also make money on any interest earned as your initial investment grows. Take a look at the chart below, which shows how $50,000 grows over 30 years. This example has 10% interest earned for the first 15 years, reduced to 7% earned the next ten years, and then down to a modest and conservative 5% interest earned per year for the last five years. This reflects the advice to reduce risk as you get closer to retirement age. See how our $50,000 grew to $514,000 over 30 years' time.

Year	Starting $	10% interest earned/year	Ending $
1	$50,000.00	$5,000.00	$55,000.00
2	$55,000.00	$5,500.00	$60,500.00
3	$60,500.00	$6,050.00	$66,550.00
4	$66,550.00	$6,655.00	$73,205.00
5	$73,205.00	$7,320.50	$80,525.50
6	$80,525.50	$8,052.55	$88,578.05
7	$88,578.05	$8,857.81	$97,435.86

8	$97,435.86	$9,743.59	$107,179.44
9	$107,179.44	$10,717.94	$117,897.38
10	$117,897.38	$11,789.74	$129,687.12
11	$129,687.12	$12,968.71	$142,655.84
12	$142,655.84	$14,265.58	$156,921.42
13	$156,921.42	$15,692.14	$172,613.56
14	$172,613.56	$17,261.36	$189,874.92
15	$189,874.92	$18,987.49	$208,862.41
		7% interest earned/Year	
16	$208,862.41	$14,620.37	$223,482.78
17	$223,482.78	$15,643.79	$239,126.57
18	$239,126.57	$16,738.86	$255,865.43
19	$255,865.43	$17,910.58	$273,776.01
20	$273,776.01	$19,164.32	$292,940.33
21	$292,940.33	$20,505.82	$313,446.16
22	$313,446.16	$21,941.23	$335,387.39
23	$335,387.39	$23,477.12	$358,864.50
24	$358,864.50	$25,120.52	$383,985.02
		5% interest earned/Year	
25	$383,985.02	$19,199.25	$403,184.27
26	$403,184.27	$20,159.21	$423,343.48
27	$423,343.48	$21,167.17	$444,510.66
28	$444,510.66	$22,225.53	$466,736.19
29	$466,736.19	$23,336.81	$490,073.00
30	$490,073.00	$24,503.65	$514,576.65

Higher-risk stocks generally earn a higher interest rate. A higher interest rate means that you have the potential to earn more money; HOWEVER, it also means you have a higher potential to lose money. So, be careful! The values of diversified stocks generally increase and decrease continuously over the years. Over the years in most cases, the value will go up overall, similar to the simplified graph shown below.

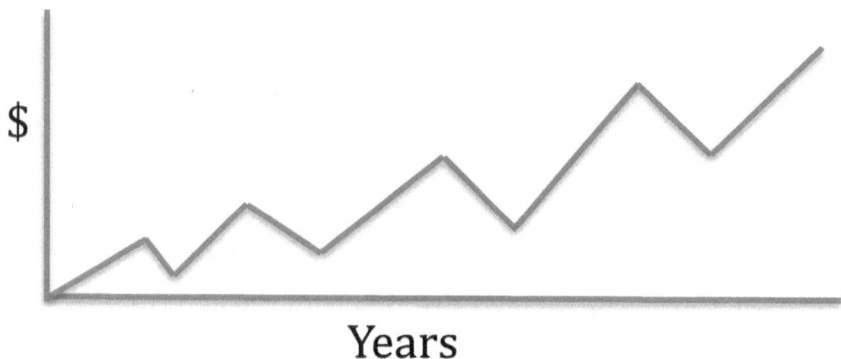

Years

When you are young, you have more time to weather the ups and downs of the stock market. This is because you have time to allow the investment to go through its ups and downs (but ultimately grow). You can therefore afford to invest in higher-risk stocks. This is why our example shows 10% interest earnings for the first 15 years (with higher-risk stocks).

As you get older and closer to retirement age, you want to protect your investments, that is, reduce the risk of loss. This is done by changing the investments to lower-risk stocks. Yes, this reduces your potential earnings, but later in life it is more important to reduce potential losses. In this hypothetical case, we changed to lower-risk investments which earned 7% interest for years 16 through 25, and then changed to even lower-risk investments which earned 5% interest for years 26 to 30.

So, that being said, if you must borrow money and take on a debt to purchase a car, purchase a car that you can afford and still allows you to meet your financial goal. Remember that decisions you make now can determine whether you are able to retire younger or will be working until you are 75 years old.

Now, if you must borrow money for a car, here is a basic guideline for auto loans:

- Put at least a 20% down payment on the car. This means you have to come up with 20% of the cost of the car in cash.
- If buying a used vehicle, take into consideration the age of the car. Make sure the life expectancy of the car is longer than the length of the loan. It is lousy to make car payments on a car that no longer runs.
- Monthly car costs should not be more than ten percent of your income. Remember that costs include not only your monthly payment (which includes interest), but also insurance, registration, tires, and

maintenance costs. If you buy a used car, give yourself a bigger budget for repairs.

If you can't meet these guidelines, wait until you can save more money for a down payment or choose a less expensive car (or get a better paying job!). Currently, a typical car loan interest rate is around 5% to 10% a year. At 5% this means that for every $1,000 you borrow; you will pay $50 each year in interest. Say you borrow $20,000; this amounts to $1000 in interest per year. For a six-year loan, this means you will pay a whopping $6,000 in interest alone. Once again, ouch!

Therefore, if it is possible to wait (if you have a car already, and it won't fall apart, or if you can use other transportation), have patience. It is better to save the money and pay cash for the car. You will end up saving thousands of dollars. It pays to have patience and discipline!

Now that I have tried to discourage you from buying an expensive car and taking out a car loan, here are more things you will need if you do take out a car loan:

- Insurance. Remember that the cost of insurance on a new car is considerably more than insurance on an older car. Get quotes from insurance companies before you commit to buying that beautiful new car you have your eye on. You can often get estimates online.
- Steady income. This often means you have worked at your current place of employment for at least two years, and you have a job history of working consistently.
- Acceptable debt-to-income ratio. That is, how much do you owe others, in respect to your income? For example, if you owe $20,000 on your credit cards and earn $30,000 a year, this means your debt is high compared to your income, and your debt-to-income ratio is not favorable.
- Acceptable credit score. Do you have a good record of paying off debts? The higher the credit score, the better the chance that the loan will be paid which makes the lenders more likely to approve your loan. Also, your credit score will affect your interest rate.

In the following chapters, we will go over some more lessons:

- How to create a budget
- How to calculate whether or not you can afford that car payment. Also, what payment amount can you handle?

That economy car is sounding pretty good now, isn't it?

CHAPTER 12
CREATING A BUDGET

Creating a budget takes some work, but it is well worth it. It may sound complicated, but if you follow the steps, it is not too difficult if you have a calculator to add, subtract, multiply, and divide (hooray for the calculator!). A computer program or spreadsheet such as QuickBooks, Excel, or Google Sheets (free) makes it even easier.

A budget will help you to determine how much money you can spend (or not spend) each month so that you may meet your goals. It's very important to do this before making any large purchases, such as a house or car. Creating a budget is also necessary for long term financial planning.

<u>Steps to Create a Budget</u>

The first step is to make a list of categories for monthly expenses. Here are some examples:

<u>Categories</u>
- Food - Groceries
- Meals out - Fast food or restaurants
- Rent or mortgage payment
- Utilities - water, gas, electricity, garbage removal
- Cell phones
- Auto Insurance
- Homeowners' or renters' insurance
- Medical insurance
- Gasoline
- Clothing
- Gifts
- Vacation/Travel

- Automotive expenses such as loan payments, registration fees, maintenance
- Medical expenses
- Tuition
- Home supplies like toilet paper, soap, laundry detergent, etc.
- Taxes - property, income, capital gains, etc.
- Child support or alimony
- Storage unit rental
- Miscellaneous

Then, under each category, list everything you spend money on throughout the year. Be sure to include expenses which don't occur every month, such as insurance or taxes. If possible, use a computer program or spreadsheet. Keep track of and write down everything you purchase or spend money on, no matter how small the amount. You will be surprised at how much you spend on small-dollar items each month. Those $5 Happy Meals really add up at the end of the month!

Keep track of everything you pay for by cash, checks, credit cards, electronic transfers, or any other method. Your check register and credit card statement may be helpful.

For items which are paid only once a year or once every few months, calculate what the amount would be per month.

Examples:

- If you pay $1,000 in car insurance every six months, then $1,000 divided by 6 months is $167 per month, so you need to save $167 each month for car insurance. Document this on your list or spreadsheet.
- If you pay $10,000 per year in property taxes, then $10,000 divided by 12 months is $833 each month, so you need to save $833 each month for property taxes. Document it on your list or spreadsheet.

After you determine all your expenses for one month:

1. Add all the expenses to determine the total dollar amount spent each month.
2. Determine your income. Add the amounts from paychecks and any other income, such as interest from the bank, stock dividends, alimony payments received, child support payments received, social security, royalties, etc.

3. Subtract the expenses from the income. If you have a positive number, this is the amount you can save each month. If you have a negative number, this is the amount of debt you have each month.

Now, look at the list of expenses:

1. Carefully go over each category and determine which expenses you can reduce or cut.
2. Then, for each category, give yourself an allowance to spend each month. For example, if you spent $200 on fast food last month, can you reduce it to $100 and increase your grocery bill by $50? If so, you can save $50 a month. It may not sound like a lot, but that would save $600 a year!
3. If you have a savings goal, determine how much money you must save each month to reach your goal. For example, if you want to save $20,000 for that down payment, maybe you can save $1,000 per month for 20 months. Or $500 per month for 40 months.

Figure out what your goals are, what your expenses will be and which expenses you can control, reduce, or cut. Then, you can figure out how long it will take to reach your goal. Adjust accordingly. You may have to downsize the house or give up something on the expense side. It will be difficult to give things up, but only you can decide what your priorities are. Make a choice: Buying your own home or have the fancy cell phone, clothes, car, etc.? Hmm, no one said this was going to be easy. Good goals are worth the sacrifice!

Cutting back on spending and sticking to a budget takes discipline, but the end result is worth it. How much is your freedom and sanity worth to you? How about eliminating the arguments between you and your significant other? Will this go a long way to reduce stress in your relationship? How much is having a roof over the heads of your family worth to you? You get the picture. The stakes are high and so are the rewards. A little discipline and sacrifice. Okay, maybe a lot of discipline and sacrifice, depending on your situation.

What Can I Do to Save Money?

Remember that saving is possible when you spend less than you make. It is usually easier to reduce expenses than it is to find a higher-paying job or get better returns on your investments (if you can afford to invest in anything!)

This is the time to look very carefully again at the categories you wrote down when creating your budget. Make every effort to see if there is any way to reduce expenses.

Re-evaluate what you really need versus what you want. Here are some common things that can be reduced or eliminated:

- Big House or Apartment (more space for junk!)
  Can you downsize your home or apartment?

- Living in an expensive neighborhood
  Can you move to a less expensive neighborhood without risking the safety of your family?

- Food Expenses
  Can you learn to cook and eat more at home instead of going out to eat so much? (Cooking is fun!) There are also differences in prices at various supermarkets. Discount markets can save you a lot of money.

There is a discount market near our home where we routinely save between 50%-75% over the big-name supermarkets. This can be a huge savings over a year's time!

- Expensive Restaurants (So yummy, but do I need the extra calories?)
  When you do go out, can it be to a less expensive restaurant? Can you eat less prime rib and more chicken?

- New and/or Expensive Car (So cool, but a less expensive car will still get me to work and may be more practical.)
  Can you make do with a more economical car? It will save on fuel, maintenance and insurance. If you have two cars; do you need both of them? Can you or your significant other carpool? Can you walk, bike, or take public transportation to work?

- Luxury Items
  Can you eliminate or reduce some of your luxury items? Can you upgrade your cell phone every five years instead of every year or two?

- Clothing (Designer labels are overrated!)
  Can you make do with less expensive clothing? Can you shop at Target or Walmart instead of Nordstrom? Can you shop on Amazon? (I like to say, "If Amazon does not sell it, you don't need it."!)

- Expensive Vacations (So fun, but can you really afford it?)
  Can you vacation locally or go camping instead of going on the fancy European vacations or cruises? Can you drive instead of fly? Can you stay in a less expensive motel instead of a luxury hotel?

- Kids (Even the kids need to sacrifice. Better yet, put them to work!)
  Can you cut down on their allowance, or can they get a job? Can you cut down on the amount you spend for their clothes and other necessities? Do your kids really need their own cars? Do the kids really need the latest video game(s) and the latest smartphone?

- Insurance (Changing policies can save you bucks!)
  Can you get a higher deductible for your health, automobile, and homeowner's insurance? Can you afford the higher deductible if you need to make a claim? If you create a large enough emergency fund then you can afford the higher deductible and in the long run save money. Shop around! Get quotes from different insurance companies.

- Education (The university diploma does not say which community college you attended prior to transferring to the university.)

Can you or your kids go to public school instead of private school? Can you or your kids go to a community college and then transfer to a university after two years? Sometimes, colleges prefer transfers because it shows a track record of completing college level classes.

- Expensive gifts (So generous but is it necessary?).
  Can you cut your budget for gifts purchased for friends and relatives? If you have a big family, this cost can be substantial. I remember in my first marriage, our Christmas gift list had over 50 people on it. Talk about holiday stress!

Other Items:

- Expensive toys such as off-road vehicles, boats, and RVs Fun, but is it worth the cost?)
- Manicures/pedicures/massages (Real beauty is on the inside, not the outside)
  Can you do your own manicures and pedicures?
- Expensive meats and seafood (So delicious! Well, yes, so splurge once in a while, not every day.)
- Shopping at large-volume warehouse stores to buy items that you will never use (Will you really save money by supersizing?). It's easy to go to Costco with the intention to purchase only a few items but end up spending $200!
- New computer (Is the old one truly too slow, or is it really okay?) Next to a new car, the only thing that depreciates as fast is a new computer. If you upgrade, make sure you really need to.
- If you pay for a storage unit which is full of junk or items you will never use, get rid of it! We have a friend who kept items he never used in a storage unit for over 25 years. Over the 25 years he paid more than $50,000! One day he took inventory and threw out everything in storage and discontinued the rental. Sometimes it's more cost effective to replace items than to store them.
- Expensive wine and spirits
  There are some pretty great inexpensive wines available now.
- Expensive memberships and/or lessons at health clubs or gyms (Got to look good and develop my spirit!). Can you find a less expensive alternative? Can you exercise on your own? Can you walk or bike with a friend? Can you purchase instructional videos? Check out YouTube; there are many instructors who have exercise and yoga classes, and they are free!

Get creative. Methods to save money are as diverse as the things you spend money on. I'm sure you can come up with more ideas than those mentioned here. Where there is a will, there is a way. Don't worry about what others will think if you get caught shopping at that discount store. Guess what? You'll be surprised to see that smart wealthy shoppers shop there, too.

CHAPTER 13
DISCIPLINE AND DELAYED GRATIFICATION

Delayed Gratification

The current society has conditioned us to enjoy instant gratification, so it is very hard for us to wait for things we want. We are hit with constant advertising telling us that we "need" this or we "need" that. Our financial system is tailored to accommodate our desire to get what we want immediately, by making it easy to obtain credit (to the detriment of the consumer). Although my family was poor when I was young, I was a spoiled child, and I remember actually feeling internal pain and anxiety when I could not have something I wanted. It was often some toy advertised on television while I was watching cartoons, and I felt I "had to have it".

It is said that "the only difference between men and boys is the price of their toys". This is true in a lot of ways. Many men like sports cars, expensive trucks and SUVs, boats, expensive sporting goods, watches, etc. I am sure if most men had the money, they would buy season tickets for their favorite sports teams as well.

The problem is when, instead of saving for the things they want and budgeting for them, many people go into debt to make the purchase. Some look only at the monthly payment to determine whether or not they can afford it. They don't look at the long-term implications of paying high interest rates (which make lender rich, not you). The interest you pay could instead be money in your savings or retirement account, but ONLY IF YOU ARE ABLE TO DELAY THE PURCHASE. This is what is meant by "delayed gratification". If it is worth having, then it is worth saving for. Don't give more money to the banks, and don't dig yourself a deeper debt hole than you can climb out of.

All of this takes discipline. Take control of your actions by holding off on spending. It's not easy, but think of your long-term goals and how much better your life will be without debt; this can be your motivation. Paying off your mortgage, early retirement, enjoying nice vacations, buying nice jewelry, and buying a nice car are all within your reach if you have the discipline AND the desire to plan before you spend. Think of accomplishing your long-term financial goals, knowing that purchases you make now may adversely affect those long-term goals. You can splurge a little bit once in a while but do so only AFTER your bills are paid and after you verify that future expenses and savings are covered. If you splurge, save the money for the expense first. Save your budgeted amount for living expenses, retirement, and any other large expenses you may have looming in the future (such as your children's college tuition).

<u>Image and Insecurity:</u>

Many people are insecure and don't even know it. Insecurity is the reason many people spend a lot of money on things, in an attempt to promote a desired image to others and influence how others think of them. I remember a quote from the TV show "The Sopranos". One of the mob bosses said, "Man is driven by his insecurities".

There are some people who don't have a great deal of money and don't spend much for upkeep and maintenance on their homes, but they drive expensive luxury cars. This is often an attempt to show others that they have the money to afford a nice ride. Some people spend a lot of money on designer clothes and jewelry, as well, so they can look good. It doesn't matter to them that their real investment, their home, is where the money should be spent. A well-maintained home will appreciate in value, whereas most cars and clothes and other material items will depreciate and eventually be worth nothing. It is a manifestation of insecurity that causes some people to spend money to "upgrade" their image. I know that in Japan, few people can afford to buy a home, so instead they love to spend their money on designer clothing. I read that homes are so expensive, Japan has 50-year mortgages, where children are liable for paying off their parents' debt after the parents pass!

I can use my own father as an example of how insecurity drives spending. I never knew him because he passed away when I was two years old. This is my perception of him based on stories my mother told me. My father was an auto mechanic. He owned a gas station back in the 1950's and 1960's when folks took their cars to the gas station to have mechanical problems fixed. There was no self-serve, and a gas station attendant actually pumped gas and checked under the hood to make sure the oil level was okay. Outside of work, my father was what my mom called a "clothes horse". He dressed fashionably and impeccably and spent a lot of money on nice suits and shoes. He fancied himself as a well-to-do business owner, and he wanted to shed the perceptions that others may think of him as a "grease monkey". I believe that it was insecurity and a desire to boost his image that prompted him to put so much emphasis on his appearance.

My mother told me this story: The church minister came to our apartment one evening and asked my father if he would donate money for a church project. My father, in an attempt to confirm his image of the successful businessman, gave the minister money without hesitation. This caused a big argument between my mother and father when the minister left, because my father had given away the rent money. How was the family going to pay the rent now, since he had just given all the money to the church? My father told my mom not to worry about it and that he would figure something out. My parents had no savings and were living paycheck to paycheck, the way many people live today. It is an all too common occurrence and often the norm rather than the exception. Just as with the way he dressed, I believe that my father giving away the rent money was caused by insecurity and the desire to maintain his projected image, rather than a desire to be generous to the church. It was his ego that would not allow him to say "no". Taking care of the family's necessities, such as rent and food, should always come first, but they did not in this case.

CHAPTER 14
INCREASING YOUR INCOME CHANGES THINGS

<u>Making More Money</u>

There are only 24 hours in a day. If you are paid by the hour, here are two ways to make more money:

1. Earn more money per hour:
   Since you don't have more hours in a day, make your time more valuable by getting paid more per hour. Obtaining a higher-paying job can do this. Education and a college degree can help you to qualify you for a higher paying job. Studying and obtaining certifications for career changes or elevations can raise your hourly wage. (Examples are: The nursing assistant who goes back to school to get a nursing degree or the computer support person who gets a Microsoft certification to qualify for a higher paying job in the field).

2. Work more hours:
   You can do this by working overtime, if it is available, or by working a second job. Since there are only 24 hours in a day, remember that you do need to sleep, spend time with your family, and maintain a quality of life outside of work. Working more hours has its limitations and drawbacks. Earning more money per hour is the better choice, if possible. Remember, "All work and no play makes Jack a dull boy".

Wealthy people know how to let their money work for them. If you can invest your money wisely, your earnings can grow. On the other hand, be aware that investments always carry some risk, and there is the possibility that you can lose money, as well. Back in the 1990s when technology stocks were flying high, I used money from my Individual Retirement Account (IRA) to buy Lucent stock. Lucent was owned by AT&T. I thought that Lucent was such huge and established company that it could never lose money. Boy, when the market crashed, so did Lucent. My $2,000 fell to around $40 almost overnight. It never did recover and eventually stayed well under $10 per share for the time that I owned it. Bad luck for me! It would have been better for me to purchase smaller quantities of stock in several different companies to reduce my risk and maximize the investment potential.

That being said, invest wisely and conservatively. Higher-risk investments have a higher potential to make money but also a higher risk of losing money. Likewise, lower-risk investments have a lower potential to make money but also a lower risk of losing money. Unfortunately, the risk is not always apparent or predictable, as my Lucent example demonstrates.

The general rule for investing is that that the older you are, the less risk you should take on your investments. One example is to invest in lower-risk stocks and reduce the percentage of your money invested in stocks as you get closer to retirement age, because you will have fewer working years to make up for any major downturns in the market.

A seasonal laborer is someone who works only during certain parts (or seasons) of the year. Examples are schoolteachers, agriculture workers, fishermen, and those who work at ski resorts, beaches, or other places which do business only during certain times of the year.

As an example, let's use a teacher, who we will call Megan, who works only nine months of each year and has three months off each summer. If Megan receives a paycheck only during the months she is working and does not plan for the three months each year that she will have no income, then she will be in trouble during the months she is not working. (Some teachers have the option to receive their pay over 12 months instead of nine.)

Are you familiar with the television show "Deadliest Catch"? It is a reality show which follows crab fisherman working in the hazardous waters off the Alaskan coast. The job is dangerous, stressful, and carries a high risk of injury or death, but crab boat captains can earn more than $200,000 per year, and crewmen can earn $50,000 in a three-month fishing season, with living expenses paid for while on the job. If this is the only employment someone has, he will need extra financial discipline to make the money last throughout the year or find additional employment. Imagine a young sailor/fisherman who makes $50,000 in three months and loves to party. Without financial discipline and planning, that money will be gone in a flash. But, with financial discipline and planning, he can save or invest that money. One day he may be able to buy his own fishing boat or business (or maybe something safer!), so that he can make more money in the future.

For a seasonal laborer, it is even more important to create a budget and make sure there is enough money to survive during the months when there is no work. If there is not enough money to survive through the year, an additional job may be necessary.

For jobs like these, it is even more important to create a budget and track expenses.

<u>Working for Less Pay</u>

What if you are not working and earning an income at all? Sometimes, working for less pay than what you are accustomed to is better than not working at all.

Living in Los Angeles all my life, I've known a few people who made quite a bit of money in the motion picture business. Hollywood is a tough place to make money; it's often either feast or famine. Every year, countless young people move to Hollywood with dreams of becoming stars; many find jobs as waiters or waitresses to make ends meet while they are waiting for their "Big Break". A few of the people I know were lucky and found good gigs (short term jobs) in Hollywood. They earned some very good money in a relatively short period of time. However, when those gigs were over, the big money stopped.

Now, in their mind, these friends feel that their time is very valuable -- all of the time. The problem with this is that when they were offered lower-paying gigs, they declined the offers because they thought a lower-paying job was beneath them, only to find over time that they were unable to secure another high-paying gig. They believe that they should always receive the high wages they had earned from their previous high-paying gigs. While waiting for the next big gig to come along, they racked up credit card debt and purchased cars and other items on credit, all with the belief that the next big break was just around the corner.

In the case of one friend, the big money job never came, and bankruptcy was the result. Another case involved a friend who I will call Jim. He was pretty big in Hollywood at one time; he drove a Jaguar and lived in a nice home in Hollywood. At the time, I had a low-paying job and was a struggling parent with bills to pay, so I took a second job working with computers to earn some extra money. Jim asked me to do some computer work for him, which required that I purchase expensive computer parts for his system. Well...it turned out Jim did not pay me for around nine months because he was "in between gigs" and was broke. Jim took advantage of our friendship. If I was in a situation where I could not pay, I would not ask for the work to be done in the first place. As it turns out, I had a lot more money and savings than my big time Hollywood friend had.

The takeaway lesson is that it is important to be willing to work for less money instead of going deeper into debt. Let go of your self-inflated ego. Be realistic about your situation. Don't expect a lucky windfall or expect to always receive the same income that you had generated at one time. For me, I would be willing to flip burgers before it came to the point where I could not pay my bills. My friends from the past would have been in a much better place financially if they had been willing to work for less money when the high-paying jobs stopped.

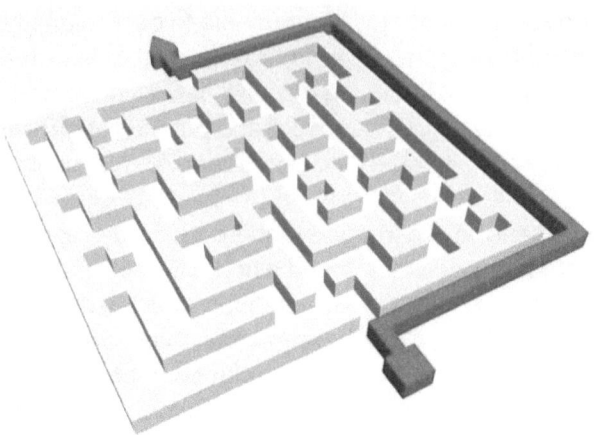

Are you in a situation where you are unable to find employment, or do you have a job that pays little money? Are you one of those who continues to pursue jobs in your field even though you have little or no luck in finding a good job? Maybe it's time to think outside the box. Look for other employment options. Do some research to find out what other kind of work may be a good fit for you. Apply for jobs outside your field even if it pays less than you are accustomed to. Lower pay is better than no pay.

Put the word out through friends and colleagues that you are looking for employment. Don't be afraid to try something new and learn new skills. You may be surprised that you enjoy working in a field you never thought about before.

CHAPTER 15
MANAGING DEBT

<u>Getting Out of Debt</u>

If people are not taught how to handle their finances and determine how much debt they can handle, they often take on more debt than they can manage. This may be one of the reasons you are reading this book. There are too many people who carry high credit card balances and purchase things way more expensive than they can afford. Are you one of them?

We know people who have difficulty putting food on the table but drive a really nice car. That nice car will eventually be worth nothing. As stated above, wouldn't it be better to buy a less expensive ride and use the extra money wisely? Money can make money. There are occasions where owning a vehicle may help you to make money, but a vehicle can be a money pit if it is not used to generate or sustain income. The value of that new ride drops the second you drive it off the lot and does not EVER stop bleeding money.

The extent of your debt and the ability or inability to pay the debt will determine how hard it is to get out of debt. The more debt you carry, the more difficult it will be to get out of debt, and the more discipline and sacrifice are needed to achieve the goal of being debt-free.

Okay, now that you have an understanding of what needs to be done, here is a plan of attack to accomplish your goal of getting out of debt. The first steps include creating a budget, as discussed in Chapter 12. It's a good idea to review that chapter before starting this process. Let's review here, too:

1. Track and categorize all your expenses for the month (you know how to do that now!).

2. Determine the amount all your expenses.

3. Determine the amount of all your sources of income.

4. Take a good, hard look at your spending categories and figure out what expenses you can eliminate or reduce. Cut back until it hurts.

5. Remember that the highest priority is to pay off your debts over everything else, especially high-interest credit card debts.

6. Don't buy anything you don't need; buy only necessities. Paying for food and rent or mortgage should be number one. Everything else comes after that. Eat less steak and eat more chicken (Isn't that what the cows say at Chick Fil A?).

7. Figure out what lifestyle changes you can make. (Don't eat out all the time, cook at home. If you don't know how to cook, check out the internet and YouTube; you CAN learn to cook!).

8. Cut out luxury items such as expensive vacations, expensive clothing and jewelry, spa and salon treatments, gym memberships, and all other items which are nice to have but are not necessities. This is a great time to give up those expensive vices such as smoking and drinking. Imagine how much you will save!

9. Once you determine which items you will no longer spend money on, add up (calculate) the new amount for all your expenses – it should now be lower!

10. Subtract your new amount for monthly expenses (the number you just calculated in step 9) from your monthly income. IF you have cut back enough on your spending and reduced your expenses, you should have a positive number. This is the amount you can put toward paying off your debt each month.

11. Divide the amount of your total debt by the amount you obtained in step 10. This will tell you how many months it will take for you to pay off your debt.

Example:
Total debt: $30,000
Amount saved to pay off debt (Step 10 above): $500 per month
$30,000 divided by $500 per month = 60 months (5 years)

Five years may seem like a long time, but guess what? Those five years will come and go no matter what. You can be in the same situation as you are now (or maybe worse), or you can be in a better place. Here is where you make a choice. You HAVE THE POWER to choose whether you will still be in debt after those five years, OR BE DEBT FREE! Ah, can you feel it now? Debt free! Reduced stress! A better life! What a glorious feeling!

If the amount of time to pay off the debt is too long, look even further for ways to pay off the debt. Is there something you can sell, such as jewelry, sports equipment, or other items? Can your family get by with one car instead of two? What about that boat, RV, or ATV? Can you sell your current car and buy a less expensive car which costs less to operate or maintain? Can you get a higher-paying job or a second job? Can you move to a less expensive home? Do the kids really need to go to that expensive private school? If your children are old enough, can they get jobs and help with expenses? (Don't spoil or enable children by giving them everything. Kids should learn to sacrifice, too; it will help them learn to become financially responsible adults.) After you've taken additional steps to generate income and/or reduce expenses, do steps 9 through 11 yet again.

12. Keep only one credit card. Use it only for emergencies. Cut up and cancel all the others.

13. Make those credit card payments even though it hurts.

14. Enjoy reduced stress as your debt gets lower and lower.

15. Do the happy dance when the debt is paid off! Hallelujah! Enjoy your life and REMAIN DEBT FREE! Don't let yourself be tempted in the future by spending money you don't have.

CHAPTER 16
REFINANCING A HOME LOAN

What Does it Mean to Refinance a Loan?

To refinance a loan is to replace an existing loan with a new loan, usually at a lower interest rate. Under certain conditions, refinancing (also called "re-fi") a loan has the potential to save you thousands of dollars. Refinancing is usually done with home loans, but you may refinance other loans, as well.

In the 2010s, interest rates dropped, in part influenced by the Federal Reserve to stimulate the economy. When the Fed lowers interest rates for lending institutions, lenders can in turn lower interest rates for the consumer.

There are several things to consider when refinancing a loan:

1. How much lower is the new interest rate than the rate on your current loan? In general, if the difference is at least one percent, a significant savings in interest may make refinancing worthwhile.

2. Do you have a home loan with an adjustable interest rate? If so, you may save money and be better off in the long run if you refinance with a fixed-rate loan. With an adjustable-interest-rate loan, your monthly payments may decrease (good thing!) or increase (bad thing!) when interest rates fluctuate. A fixed-rate loan will ensure that monthly payments will remain the same throughout the life of the loan.

3. How much do you owe on your existing loan? How long will it be before the loan is paid? If you have only five years left on a loan, you may not benefit from refinancing because fees associated with obtaining a new

loan can be several thousand dollars. If the fees exceed your savings, you will not save money by refinancing.

4. Do you have a favorable credit score? If you racked up your credit card debt and have delinquent accounts, you may not be eligible to refinance a loan.

5. How long have you lived in the home? Generally, you need to live in your home for at least one year before you benefit from a refinance.

6. How long do you plan on staying in your current home? If you plan on selling the home within a few years, then it may not pay for you to refinance. Again, loan fees may exceed the amount you will save in interest.

If your financial condition is good, you have an option to refinance with a shorter-term loan, which will save you thousands of dollars in interest. For example, if you currently have 20 years left on a 30-year loan, you can refinance with a 15-year loan. Monthly payments may be higher, but you will save thousands of dollars on interest in the end. On the other hand, if you have ten years left on your loan and refinance with a 20-year loan, you may pay more in interest in the end.

Determine if Refinancing is Worth It

Just as with any home loan, a refinanced home loan has fees associated with it. These include an application fee, appraisal fee, attorney fees, title search and insurance fees, and home inspections fees (many of these fees are known as "closing costs"). Closing costs are typically 2% to 3% of the total value of the loan. Remember, even if you obtain a loan which has a lower interest rate than your current loan, it is not worth refinancing if loan fees exceed the amount you would save in interest. If you are unsure whether or not you will save money by refinancing, do the math. Here is an example:

1. For this example, you plan to sell the home in eight years:
    8 years x 12 months = 96 months.

2. Write down your current monthly mortgage (home loan) payment. For this example, current payments are $3,000 per month.

3. Determine how much you would pay if you kept this loan and sold the home in eight years:
    96 months x $3,000 per month = $288,000
    This is the amount you would pay if you do not refinance.

4. Determine how much you would pay if you refinanced with a loan which has a lower interest rate, and then sold the home in eight years. In this example, the new monthly payment would be $2,500, based on a $300,000 loan with a 15-year fixed interest rate of 2.9%.
    96 months x $2,500 per month = $240,000

5. Determine the amount in fees associated with the new home loan. Closing costs are typically 2% to 3% of the loan amount. We will use the average, 2.5%.
    $300,000 x 0.025 = $7,500

6. Add the loan fees to the amount you obtained in number 4 above:
    $240,000 + $7,500 = $247,500.
    This is the amount you will pay over eight years if you refinance.

7. So, which is better? To refinance or not to refinance?
    Without refinance: You will pay $288,000
    With refinance: You will pay $247,500
    Savings with refinance: $288,000 - $247,500 = $40,500

You want to pay the lesser amount, so in this case, refinancing is the winner! You will save $40,500 over eight years!

This one is an easy decision. A savings of $40,500 is substantial.

If you don't have enough money to cover closing costs, an option is to include the loan fees in the loan amount. Take this into consideration when you do your calculations and see if this is a good option for you.

Refinancing can save you money, but only if certain conditions are met. Look at your situation and see if re-fi is a good option for you. It has the potential to save you a LOT of money!

Refinancing a Home Loan to Consolidate Debts

Refinancing your home can be used to pay off other debts. In this case, when obtaining a new loan, you would borrow more than the current principal amount owed on the home. In other words, you borrow against the equity that you have in your home. So, why would you increase the debt on your home? Interest rates for home loans are typically lower than interest rates on credit cards and other loans. If you pay off the other loans and consolidate those debts into your home loan, you may save money in interest. You will also simplify your debts by consolidating multiple debts into one.

Here is an example:

- You have a home loan and owe $100,000.
- You also owe $30,000 on credit cards which have an 18% interest rate (with compounded interest!), $50,000 on a student loan which has a 4% interest rate, and $4,000 on a car loan which has 5% interest rate. These debts total $84,000.
- You have the opportunity to refinance your home loan with a 3.5% interest rate.
- When refinancing the home loan, you make the new loan for $184,000 instead of $100,000. You receive $84,000 in cash and use that cash to pay off the other three loans.
- You now owe $184,000 on the new (refinanced) home loan, but you consolidated four loans into one – one with a lower interest rate, significantly lower in the case of the credit cards.

You must be careful when consolidating loans. Remember that even if you reduce an interest rate on a loan by consolidating, you likely will extend the time it takes to pay off the loan. A short-term loan becomes a long-term loan. This means you will pay interest for a longer period of time.

For instance, in the example above, if you determine that it will take you 15 years to pay off the $30,000 credit card bill (at 18% interest!), you certainly would pay less interest and save a substantial amount of money by consolidating the credit card balance into a 15-year home loan. On the other hand, if the $4,000 car loan is scheduled to be paid off in four years (at 5% interest) and you consolidate it into a 15-year home loan (at 3.5% interest), you may actually end up paying more in interest over time. Before making the decision to consolidate the car loan into the refinanced home loan, determine how much interest you would pay with by sticking with your current loan and how much interest you would pay if you consolidated. On-line calculators are available to help you do this.

So, if you use this method only to consolidate debts and pay less in interest, and NOT as a tool to enable you to rack up more credit card debt, it can be a smart move. You will save a significant amount of money on interest. In addition, interest paid on a home loan is tax deductible. More savings!

<u>Refinancing to Obtain Cash for Other Items</u>

There are other reasons to obtain extra cash when refinancing a home loan. Some people use the available cash to do home improvements, renovations, or room additions. In some cases, this can be a smart move. If the improvements increase the value of your home, it may be worth it. For example, if you have a three-bedroom, one-bathroom house and you use the extra cash to add a second bathroom, this will usually increase the resale value of your home.

113

Adding that second bathroom will also make your home easier to sell in the future. Just make sure the increase in home value is higher than the amount you spend on renovations.

Sometimes, renovations are necessary even if the cost exceeds the increased value of a home. A new roof is a good example. The cost for a new roof may exceed the added value to the home, but it is a necessary expense and can save you a big repair bill from future water damage. In this case, refinancing your home so that you have money for a new roof may be a good idea.

If you refinance your home to obtain money for a new car (just because you want it), boat, or RV, or for an expensive vacation, this is NOT a good use of the money. The car, boat, and RV will only cost you money and will lose value. The vacation is not an investment at all.

On the other hand, if you refinance your home and use extra cash to purchase a car because you really need it, this changes things. You might save by using the re-fi money instead of taking out a car loan. Remember to calculate how much interest you would pay with both loans before deciding which is the better way to go.

Remember, there are a number of refinance calculators available online, often provided by lending institutions. Everyone's situation is different. Put your information into the calculator to see if a re-fi will work to your advantage.

CHAPTER 17
STAYING OUT OF DEBT

Once you are out of debt, the best thing to do is to stay out of debt. If you are not in debt now, keep it that way! At the very least, be at a debt level that you can handle. You should incur debt for necessities only, not for luxury items. If you do choose to take on a debt for a luxury item, it is best if that item will increase in value over time (such as a vacation home). Remember, you can still buy luxury items, but the purchase has to be budgeted for.

<u>Plan Ahead to Stay Out of Debt</u>

We've talked about most of these things already, but it doesn't hurt to go over them again:

1. By now, you should have created a budget as described in Chapter 12. If you determine that you will have money left over each month after paying all your expenses, this is great! This is the money you can save and/or spend on other stuff.

2. Make a list of all your known future expenses, such as replacing an old car, home maintenance (new roof or plumbing?), school tuition, weddings, medical bills, etc.

3. It is important to have enough savings to cover both expected and unexpected expenses (more on this in Chapter 19). Unexpected expenses are bound to occur: You crash your car and need to replace it. The plumbing needs repairs. You become ill or injured and are unable to work, or you lose your job. Put as much money into your savings account each month as possible, and plan to have enough

savings so that you can pay for expected expenses. This way, you don't have to incur debt when unexpected expenses arise.

4. Do you have enough money to pay all expenses and put into your savings each month? If so, you are in good shape. If not, look at your expenses and do what you can to reduce them (see Chapters12 and 15).

5. If you have kids, put them on a budget, as well. Figure out how much you can cut back in spending on the kids. For parents who want to give their children everything, this can be one of the hardest things to do. However, remember that it is not worth spoiling your children if it is beyond your financial means. Your obligation is to feed them and put a roof over their head. Nowhere does it say that children have to live in luxury, have their own new cars, wear the latest and greatest fashions and buy a new smartphone every year. Remember, if you lose your home, your kids are homeless too!

6. Use credit cards for convenience and emergencies only. Use a credit card that does not charge a fee just to have the card. Pay off the balance each month in full so that you don't pay interest or fees. Get a credit card which accrues points, pays an annual rebate, or gives airline miles (if you travel) whenever you use it.

7. Instead of obtaining a loan to purchase a car, RV, boat, television, or any luxury item, save the money FIRST and pay cash for the item. You will save hundreds or thousands of dollars by not paying interest. Just think what you can do with that extra few hundred or thousand dollars. Delayed gratification pays!

8. If your current income is not adequate, consider making more money by getting a better job or a second job, or going back to school for a degree and/or certification which can make your time more valuable. Figure out what your new salary COULD be and see if this would help you to meet your financial goals and keep you out of debt. If you want to go back to school or get a certification, figure out what it will cost, taking into consideration that you may have a reduced income if you must work fewer hours while attending school. But be careful! Don't incur so much debt on an education that it you make your situation worse. Make sure your prospective field is in demand and you can easily secure a job. It can be catastrophic to take on a large education debt, only to find that you cannot get a job in your chosen field and pay down the debt.

9. Remember always to live within your means. Don't fall into the trap of instant gratification or keeping up appearances when you cannot afford it. The stress created by heavy debt can ruin your life and the lives of your family. Take a moment and think how wonderful and blissful it would be to have control of your financial situation and to be free of financial and emotional stress. Or, maybe to retire early? Ahhh, doesn't that sound good?

CHAPTER 18
GOALS

Smart Goals Versus Not-so-Smart Goals

People work better and smarter if they have a goal. Maybe your goal is to get out of debt. Maybe your goal is to improve your living conditions and buy a better house in a better neighborhood. Maybe it's to take time off work or reduce your work hours so you can go back to school or spend time with your family. Maybe you want to get rid of that old junker car and buy a better new or used car. There are smart goals, and there are goals that are not so smart. A goal which leads to a poor financial situation is not smart.

An example of a smart goal would be to purchase something that will either retain or increase its value. For instance, purchasing an affordable home in a good neighborhood is usually a good investment because it will always be worth SOMETHING. If the economy takes a dive, there is a chance that a home could become worth less than what you paid for it, but it will always be worth something (and the value will likely increase again when the economy improves). Purchasing the home would be money well invested, as your money would be spent on something tangible which will retain or increase its value. (Make sure to get that home inspection before you buy! You don't want any unexpected expenses to repair something you didn't know about beforehand.)

Examples of not-so-smart goals are to purchase a vehicle, boat, RV, or expensive home that you cannot afford. As mentioned in previous chapters, one of the worst financial investments is a new car because the value of a new car drops the second you drive it off the car lot and continues drop every year until the car is worth next to nothing. The same holds true for most boats, RVs, and other "toys".

You must decide what is more important to you. You work hard for your money. If you can save $25,000, do you want to spend it now, or do you want to invest it and watch it grow?

Make a list of your goals and then create a plan to achieve those goals. As you achieve your goals, you can create new goals. Once you are out of debt and in good financial standing, you may be able to get that fancy car, after all!

Step-By-Step Plan To Save for A Goal

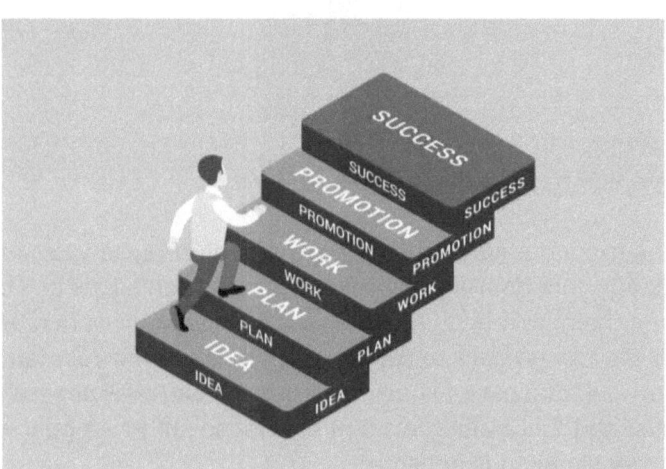

As discussed in previous chapters, the first goals are to eliminate debt, gain control of your finances, and have enough savings to cover any unplanned expenses. Once you have accomplished this, it is time to create new goals (that is, planned expenses) and create a plan to achieve them. Here are some steps to help you do this:

1. Make a list of your financial goals and prioritize them. Everyone has different goals. Maybe you want to purchase a home. Pay school tuition. Pay for your child's wedding. Buy that fancy car, RV, furniture, or a computer. Maybe you want to retire early. The list goes on. What goals are most important to you?

2. Do some research to determine how much your goal is going to cost. Remember to include additional costs (taxes, insurance, maintenance, accessories, etc.).

3. Figure out how many months you need to achieve the goal. For example, if you may expect your car to last two more years (24 months), and then you will buy another one. Or, you just had a baby, so you have about 18 years to save for college tuition.

4. Determine how much you need to save each month to reach your goal. To do this, divide the total cost by the number of months you need to save. For Examples:
   a. You plan to pay $15,000 for a used car in two years (24 months). $15,000 divided by 24 months means you will need to save $625 each month for two years.
   b. You plan to pay $100,000 for your child's college tuition in 18 years (216 months). $100,000 divided by 216 months means you will need to save $463 each month for 18 years. (This does not take into account any interest that your savings may accrue, nor does it take into account any potential losses due to an investment gone bad. This means you may end up with more money or less money depending on how this savings is invested).

5. Start saving! Use your new-found skills to remain debt-free and to put the pre-determined amount of money into your savings each month. Sometimes, it is a good idea to open a separate savings account just for a specific goal. If you are able, put even a little extra into the savings account. The more you save each month, the faster you will obtain your goal! The faster you obtain your goal, the sooner you can start saving for your next goal.

6. Once you save enough money, you can make your purchase when appropriate. Remember, do your best not to incur debt to reach your goal.

Enjoy the reward of your discipline and planning. Celebrate! Yessss!

CHAPTER 19
PAYING FOR COLLEGE

One of the biggest expenses facing parents and students today is paying for college. In 2018, the average cost for a student to attend an in-state public university in California was $21,000, and $47,000 to attend a private university (this includes tuition, fees, and room and board). Add the cost of books, supplies, and other living expenses over four years, and you can be looking at costs of $100,000 to $200,000 or more PER CHILD! And that's not even counting graduate school. Every year this amount increases.

So, how on earth is a person supposed to pay such a large amount of money? The first way is for parents to start saving money for their children's college as soon as the child is born. This way, you will have 18 years to save and invest the money. For young parents, this can be difficult or impossible to do. Often, parents start saving too late, or they don't save at all because they don't plan for the future. For children of parents who cannot afford to pay for college, they must find a way to pay for college themselves. My wife an example. She was one of six children in a single-income family. There was no way her parents could afford to save enough to pay for all six kids to go to college, and each child was expected to pay their own way. Growing up with this expectation, my wife was completely unaware that many parents pay for their children's college education. My wife went to college, worked at the same time to pay the tuition, and raised two children. During this time she was a single parent. Talk about difficult!

To repeat my former boss' quote, "The only way to get ahead in this world is to get a good education so you can get a good job so you can AFFORD to save money. If you can AFFORD to save money, then you can afford to open your own business, which is one ticket to financial freedom."

Well, my daughter's mother and I started saving for our daughter's college right after she was born, BUT... it still was not enough. We did not do the math and only saved what we thought we could afford without creating an actual budget. We ended up getting lucky in that my daughter was a stellar student and received a great academic scholarship, and we also received some unexpected financial aid.

<u>Financial Aid:</u>

Here is something I did not know when I applied to college myself. I was accepted to the University of Southern California (USC) School of Engineering and to the University of California at Los Angeles (UCLA). At the time (many moons ago), USC tuition was $10,000 per year, and UCLA tuition was $1,200 per year. My family could not afford the USC tuition, so I went to UCLA. Financial aid is available to low-income students who qualify, but I had no idea what financial aid was all about. Part of the financial aid for some colleges and universities include work programs, where students can work at an on-campus job, allowing them to earn money and reduce tuition costs. My mother was a single parent and had a low-paying job. I would have qualified for financial aid, but at the time I did not know it existed.

Two sources of financial aid are grants and scholarships. Grants and scholarships are FREE money, sometimes called "gift aid" because the money is given to the recipient and does not have to be paid back. Grants are usually based on a student's need, whereas scholarships are based on a student's merit (achievements). There are thousands of companies and organizations who give money to college students. It's up to you to search for them (hooray for the internet!) and apply for them (make sure to apply by the deadline!)

One source for grants and scholarships is the U.S. Department of Education. On their website, you can find a Free Application for Federal Student Aid (FAFSA). You use this application to apply for financial aid for college or graduate school. Students should complete the FASFA even if they don't qualify. This is because if parents become disabled or unable to work, the student may then become eligible for the financial aid. If this should happen, and the student has not already submitted an application, he or she have to wait until the following year to apply. Submitting the application is a lot of work and very financially invasive (invasive like a financial colonoscopy!), but it is worth it. When submitting an application, you must also submit a copy of your current tax return. Also, a new application must be submitted each year. FAFSA is something you may not need but it is good insurance to have just in case.

When my daughter was 16 years old, she did not have a job. We told her that her job was to find and apply for grants and scholarships. She did not take us seriously and as a result did not receive any grant money. She did, however, obtain a great academic scholarship which paid a portion of her tuition at Smith College in Massachusetts. The scholarship paid about $15,000 of her $40,000 tuition each year, which helped considerably.

(Smith College is a women's college; it is a great school and was the perfect fit for my daughter. Sylvia Plath, Barbara Bush, and Julia Child are a few of the many famous women who attended school there. It is not well known on the West Coast but is very well known on the East Coast.)

Student Loans:

Another option to pay for college is to obtain a student loan. Student loan interest rates are usually low, and you don't have to start paying them back until you graduate from college.

Caution! Be careful not to borrow too much for an education. Remember that it's important to obtain a college degree which will allow a student to earn enough money to repay the loan, in addition to all other expenses. Unfortunately, it is a growing trend for students to take on enormous debt to obtain a college or post-graduate degree. Many students believe that they will obtain a high-paying job immediately after college, only to find this is not always true. Some students find themselves paying off student loans for ten years or more. Other students obtain college degrees in subjects that interest them but find it difficult to get a job in their desired field after graduation.

<u>Community Colleges</u>

One way to reduce the cost of a college education is to attend a community college for the first two years, and then transfer to a university for the remaining two years. The cost of a community college is far less than that of a university, and you will save a significant amount of money. When you graduate from the university, the diploma will have the name of the university on it; it does not say on the diploma that you attended the university for only two years.

CHAPTER 20
EMERGENCY FUNDS AND UNEXPECTED EVENTS

Emergency Funds

A goal everyone should have is to establish an emergency fund (savings for unexpected expenses). A good rule is to have an amount between two and nine months of your normal income. There is a huge difference between two and nine months worth of income, and the amount you choose to keep in your emergency fund depends on a number of factors.

One factor is your earning potential. If you should lose your job unexpectedly, how easy would it be to get a new job based on the job market and your job skills? Whether your job skill is in high or low demand will often determine how easy or difficult it will be to get a new job. Here are some considerations on how much you should have in your emergency fund in case you lose your job, are unable to work, or want to quit your job in the future. Which category are you in? What category can you be in if you obtain additional education and/or training?

Finding a new job would be:

- Easy:
  I can easily find a job with similar or better pay.
- Average:
  I have good qualifications, but it will take a while to find a new job.
- Fairly difficult:
  Finding work for similar pay is limited. There are either few jobs and/or there is a lot of competition for those jobs.
- Very difficult:

I don't have the right job skills, or I work in a specialized field with limited demand. It will be difficult and take a long time to get a job with a similar salary.

What would you do if you had a long-term illness or disability? These types of things are impossible to predict and having an emergency fund can make the difference between eating and starving or between keeping or losing your home. If you are a parent or the sole household bread winner, your responsibilities are even greater, as you have a family to support, so the emergency fund becomes even more important. Once your debts are paid, establishing an emergency fund should a high-priority goal. Consider it an important type of life insurance -- insurance for while you are living, rather than insurance in case of death.

Unexpected Events

In addition to unexpected expenses, there can be unexpected events or disasters which have a financial impact. Unexpected events include any number of things, including fire, earthquakes, hurricanes, unplanned pregnancy, accidents, injuries, epidemics, and more.

An example of an unexpected event is the Coronavirus (COVID-19) pandemic in 2019-2020. The epidemic created devastating health, social, and financial crises worldwide. In an effort to control the spread of disease, "social distancing" (where people are required to maintain a physical distance from one another) and quarantines became mandatory. Many businesses were required by law to close. Millions of people were without jobs: Restaurant workers, public transportation drivers, manufacturing workers, airline workers, cruise line workers, and many more. The list is endless. Schools were closed, and children were homeschooled and taught remotely via teleconferencing.

No one saw the pandemic coming, and few were prepared, physically or financially, when it occurred. Businesses which had been flourishing quickly became insolvent. The stock market crashed at levels never before seen in history. Pandemics had occurred previously throughout history, but an event of this magnitude had not happened before. At one time, the price of oil was even less than $0.00! People lined up at grocery stores. There was a shortage of toilet paper -- people were afraid that they would run out of it if they had to stay at home in quarantine for prolonged periods of time. Prior to this pandemic, the hysteria and hoarding of goods were seen only in towns which expected a disaster such as a hurricane. An event like this had never happened on nation-wide or global levels like this before. I kept thinking I would wake up one morning to find out it was all a bad dream. It was like something right out of the old TV series "The Twilight Zone" or the newer series "Black Mirror".

Individuals and businesses were unable to pay their rent, and emergency laws were put into place to prevent evictions. However, preventing the evictions did not erase the debts; it only postponed payment of the debt. In most cases, interest on the debt continued to accrue, so debts actually increased. The United States Government passed a two-TRILLION-dollar bill to provide financial aid to companies, and more similar bills followed. Taxpayers whose income was below a certain level received money from the government. As of this writing, the national debt is well over 20 trillion dollars, and this crisis will add greatly to this number. (The national debt is borrowed money. There is a possibility that this debt may never be paid, leading to an eventual financial collapse, but that is a topic for another book...)

This is an example an emergency fund with enough to cover nine months may not be enough. At the time of this writing, the COVID-19 crisis is still in full swing. Many businesses will remain closed permanently even after the crisis subsides, which means many no longer have their jobs. There will be long-term impacts on financial and social situations; bankruptcies and suicides will be consequences of this pandemic, just as they were after the stock market crash of the 1920's.

Those who had large emergency funds were better able to weather the financial storm associated with this event. There are those who are prepared and keep extra supplies in case of an earthquake, tornado, hurricane, or other disaster, but few expected a financial crisis as deep reaching as the Coronavirus pandemic. A huge lesson was learned by this event, and the world will be changed forever after.

Hope for the best but prepare for the worst!

CHAPTER 21
UNFORESEEN MAJOR EXPENSES

Forewarning! This is not a fun topic, but it is an important one. We may do our best to plan for our future, but life often throws unexpected and unplanned situations our way. Here are a few.

Boomerang Children

A trend we see today is that many in the "Baby Boomer" generation are supporting three adult generations: Themselves, elderly parents, and adult children.

Adult children who leave their parents' home and then later return are known as "boomerang kids". They leave but find they are unable to afford living on their own, so they return, just like a boomerang. The inability to live on their own is due to factors that we've discussed before, such as increasing costs for education, rent, and home ownership (especially in high-demand urban areas), and the inability to find employment.

Many young people today believe and expect that they will get a high-paying job immediately out of college and are disappointed to find that this often is not the case. My friend's son is an example. He received a bachelor's degree in computer game design. He had high hopes to work in the gaming industry and make good money, just like the designers of games such as "Call of Duty" or "Fortnite". He was not aware how difficult it is to obtain a job in this field. After graduating college and a long period of unsuccessful job interviews, he ended up moving back in with his mother and finding work at a Walmart earning minimum wage.

Long-Term Care

"What kind of immortality plan do you offer?"

Another major expense is long-term care for yourself or family members who are elderly, disabled, or ill. Long-term care may occur in your home or in a facility such as a hospital, convalescent or nursing home, or a rehabilitation facility.

To give an example on the impact this can have on your finances, I will describe my mother's experience. At age 63, she became disabled by severe rheumatoid arthritis, which disfigured and limited the use of her hands and feet. Although disabled, she continued to live alone in her home, but at around age 81, she fell and broke both shoulders. She became confined to a wheelchair and recovered in a rehabilitation facility. Medicare covered the first 100 days of care in the rehabilitation facility, but she was responsible to pay the facility cost after that.

Not long after returning home, she fell again and broke her ankle. After determining that she could no longer live in her home, she moved to a nursing home. The cost of the nursing home care, medical expenses, insurance premiums, and medications were $84,000 per year.

Fortunately, long before my mother fell the first time, she had the foresight to purchase long-term care insurance and supplemental medical insurance (in addition to Medicare). After entering the nursing home, Medicare again covered the first 100 days of care. After that, the long-term care insurance covered 40% of the nursing home costs. The insurance company paid that 40% until the total money paid out hit the policy maximum of $125,000. It took only three-and-a half years to reach the limit. Medicare and the supplemental medical insurance covered some of the remaining expenses, but at the end of the day, my mother paid $42,000 out of pocket each year for the first three-and-a half years. After the long-term care insurance ran out, her out-of-pocket costs increased to $75,000 per year. At the time of her death, she had lived in the nursing home for five years and paid more than $259,000 out of pocket.

Luckily, my mother had enough savings to cover the expenses which were not covered by Medicare and the long-term care and supplemental medical insurance policies. My siblings and I were lucky that she had the insurance as well as the savings to cover these expenses. Without the insurance, she would have paid more than $400,000 for her care. Even with the insurance policies, she would have wiped out her savings had she lived another five years. My mother worked many years in healthcare. She witnessed firsthand how extensive medical bills can destroy people financially, and so had the knowledge and foresight to buy extra insurance. This planning enabled her to keep her home which we still own to this day. Without my mother's foresight and planning, we would have had to sell her home to pay her medical expenses.

Other Major Medical Expenses

Severe diseases, such as cancer, can be extremely expensive to treat. The costs of therapy, medications, surgeries, and hospital stays can easily rise to hundreds of thousands of dollars. If your insurance policy has a maximum payout, you can easily reach the limit in a short time. A million-dollar maximum may seem like a lot but can quickly be reached in certain medical situations. Other chronic diseases or disabilities, such as diabetes, heart disease, blindness, or injuries can mean long-term medical care, medications, and/or therapy.

<u>In-Home Care</u>

Sometimes, receiving medical care or therapy at home is a better option than staying in a hospital or other medical facility. The cost will vary, depending on the situation. Does the patient need care four hours a day, eight hours a day, or 24 hours a day? Can he walk, feed or dress himself, or go to the bathroom by himself? Does he need administered medications or physical or occupational therapy? The more care a patient requires, the higher the cost. In some cases, the cost for in-home care may exceed the cost of a nursing home.

<u>Life Insurance</u>

"The workplace accident rider
won't kick in within the next 30 seconds."

Life insurance is not for the person who is insured. It is for the survivors (the beneficiaries) of the person who is insured. Having life insurance is especially important if you are the primary source of income for your family, and your family will need the money to survive if you should die. There are different kinds of life insurance. I will describe only two of the most common types here, term life insurance and whole life insurance.

With term life insurance, you purchase a specified amount (called the death benefit) which will be paid to your beneficiaries upon your death. The policy is for a specified amount of time, or "term". Once the term expires, you may renew it for another term. The cost (called the premium) for the insurance depends on variables such as your age, gender, health, and habits (such as smoking). For instance, a person who is young, healthy, and does not smoke will pay a lower premium than a person who is older, not healthy, and smokes. Term life insurance is more affordable than other types of life insurance. You may purchase additional insurance which will pay extra should you have an accidental death. If you stop paying the premium, insurance coverage is discontinued.

Whole life insurance is a permanent insurance policy and does not expire. In addition to the death benefit, the policy includes a tax-deferred savings account, known as the cash value. The cash value accrues interest at a fixed rate. When you pay your premium, some of the premium goes to the cash value, and the cash value grows over time. Due to these extra features and to fees associated with a whole life policy, the cost to purchase a whole life insurance policy is significantly more than the cost of a term life insurance policy.

Life insurance will help to ensure that if you should die, your family will be able to pay the rent or mortgage and other expenses. It helps to provide financial stability and lowers the chance of financial problems in the case of your death. Since the chance of death increases as we age, life insurance becomes more expensive the older we get. If you are retired, have no debt, and have a lot of money saved, then life insurance may be unnecessary.

CHAPTER 22
ON-LINE BANKING

Doing your banking online is a great convenience. It allows you to pay bills from your computer or smart device in the comfort of your own home. You don't have to write a paper check or buy stamps to mail your payments.

The way it works is to first sign onto your bank's website from your computer, and then follow the website instructions to create (register) a log-in identification (ID) and password. Once you have created an ID and password, follow the website instructions to enter your ID and password to access your account. Make sure the password is complex and not easy for someone else to guess. A combination of upper and lower-case letters along with numbers and symbols helps to make your account more secure. It is very important that you keep your ID and password confidential so that no unauthorized person can access your account.

Once you log in to your bank account, you can perform many functions. Here are just a few: Check your account balances, balance your checkbook, move funds from one account to another, deposit checks, and pay bills. Check with your bank and look through the website to see other available functions.

<u>Using Your On-Line Checking Account to Pay Bills:</u>

Previously, the most common way to pay bills was to write a paper check, put it in an envelope with a postage stamp, and send it to the recipient by U.S. Mail. Now, there are several ways you can pay bills electronically, using a computer or other smart device. Paying bills electronically is easier, faster, cheaper (no checks, envelopes, or stamps), safer (checks cannot be lost or stolen in the mail), and you receive a receipt and proof of payment immediately.

One method to pay bills is by transferring money electronically from your bank account to the recipient (the company or person who you wish to pay). When you use this method, you log into the recipient's website and access the bill-pay function. After you follow the instructions to enter your bank account information and the amount you wish to pay, the funds are transferred electronically from your account to the recipient's account. When using this method to make a payment, the payment is usually transferred to the recipient immediately. You have the option to set up your payment process on the recipient's website so that the information remains on the website, so that you don't have to re-enter it each time you want to pay a bill. You also have the option to set up automatic payments, so that payments will automatically be sent to the recipient. Be careful if you do this. You must make sure that sufficient funds are available in your account when the automatic payment occurs.

Another method to pay bills electronically is to "write" an electronic check through your on-line checking account. The initial setup for this method may be a little extra work, but this step is done only one time and makes things simple in the future. First, log in to your bank account and go to the "Bill Pay" section. The initial step is to enter the information for each recipient (e.g., the company's name and address, and your account number with that company). The information will stay in the bank's computer system, so the next time you want to send a check to that recipient, you do not need to enter this information again. Some large companies, such as utility companies, other banks, or credit card companies, will already be in the bank's computer system, so you need only to choose the company from a list and provide your account number. Some companies have more than one address, so be sure to use the appropriate address for payments. If you have more than one account at the bank (e.g., savings and checking), make sure to choose the correct account.

If the recipient is a small company or an individual, the bank's computer will generate a paper check and send it by U.S. mail, at no charge. When this is the case, there is usually a lag period of five days or so until the recipient receives the check, so be sure to take this into account when making a payment, so that your payment is received on time. For large companies, the bank will usually transfer the funds electronically, and usually the same day.

If a monthly payment is a fixed amount, such as a mortgage payment, you also have the option to set it up so that the payment is automatically sent each month, without any intervention from you. This is a good way to pay off credit card debt, to make sure that payments are on time and prevent late fees (which result in still more debt). Again, if you choose to do this, it is important to make sure there is always enough money in the account to cover the automatic payments; otherwise, you will have insufficient funds to make a payment and create overdraft problems.

Personally, I prefer to use the electronic check method to pay bills because I don't like to provide my bank account information to others. By limiting the number of people and systems that have my account information, I reduce the chance of theft or fraud.

Regarding bank statements and statements from utility companies or other companies you owe money to, you can access their individual websites and choose have statements sent to you by U.S. mail, email, or both.

It is important that EVERY time you make an on-line payment, ATM withdrawal or deposit, or any other transaction, REMEMBER TO ENTER THE TRANSACTION ON YOUR CHECKBOOK REGISTER (It's that paper book that comes with your checkbook, the one we talked about in Chapter 3), so that you keep accurate banking records and balance your checking account. If you prefer, you may use a spreadsheet or other recording method instead of the paper checkbook register.

<u>Paying Bills By Credit Card</u>

For some companies you can use a credit card to pay bills. It is similar to paying from your bank account, but instead you choose the option to pay by credit card and enter your credit card information. If you choose this method, make sure to pay your credit card balance in full each month so that you don't accrue credit card debt. Paying by credit card can be advantageous if you earn points or miles when using the card. In this case, you actually get paid to use the credit card!

CHAPTER 23
CYBER SECURITY

Electronic banking is convenient, fast, and easy. The downside is that since you are online it is critical to keep your financial accounts safe from theft. If others obtain the ability to log in to your financial accounts, they can steal your money and identity. Believe me, this will make your life miserable. Keeping your on-line accounts secure and your IDs and passwords confidential is of the utmost importance.

I have a friend who had her phone hacked. $50,000 was transferred from her bank account to an account in the Philippines. It is difficult enough to fix a problem like this within the United States but involving a foreign government and law enforcement agency makes it extremely difficult. This bad situation was eventually solved, but it took MONTHS! Good thing she did not have immediate plans for the money!

Identity theft has become one the largest threats people face today. Theft can happen in many ways and include stolen credit cards, financial information, Social Security numbers, and legal information. Here are some steps you can take to help protect your identity and bank accounts.

Secure On-Line Access

Be careful of where and how you access electronic financial accounts. It is easier for savvy computer hackers to obtain your personal information when you use a public internet connection.

- Never use a public Wi-Fi internet access when accessing any financial account. When using public Wi-Fi (such as coffee shops or restaurants, an airport, your place of employment, or any other public place), hackers have ways to obtain your log-in information and use it to gain access to your account.
- Use only a private, encrypted, and trusted Wi-Fi account, such as your home.
- If you must access a financial account while in a public place, turn off your Wi-Fi connection and use the Cellular Data connection instead; it is more secure.

Two-Step Verification

Another way to protect your financial accounts is to use a "two-step verification" process each time you log in to your account. A two-step verification means that two methods are required to verify your identity before you may access your account. The first verification method is your ID and password. The second method is to enter a special security code. This security code is a random number which is computer generated by the system you are logging into. A different code is generated each time you wish to log in to your account. Once you enter your ID and password, the bank's computer will generate the security code.

There are several ways to obtain the security code. It may be sent to you by text or email. In other cases, you will use an App on your computer or electronic device to generate the unique code. You may set up the two-step verification process when you log in to your account. You may also choose the method you would like to receive the security code.

A good, secure App is Google Authenticator; it is a free App for iPhone and Android. The App generates a new six-digit code every 30 seconds and works even if you don't have a cell signal or Wi-Fi because it works independently from the internet. You can have multiple codes for multiple accounts with different companies, and Google Authenticator will keep them all secure. IMPORTANT: If you replace your smartphone, make sure to IMMEDIATELY deactivate two-step verification on all your accounts and then re-establish it with your new phone. To prevent a big headache, don't trade in your old phone until you do this. Don't lose your cellphone, either. Recovery is possible, but it is very difficult and time consuming.

<u>Identity Theft Protection Services</u>

Identity theft protection services are companies which, for a fee, closely monitor your personal information. The company monitors your bank accounts, credit cards, loans, credit reports, and other personal information. If there is suspicious activity which indicates your personal information may be compromised, the identity protection company will alert you. In some cases, the service will lock down your account, so that no new credit card accounts may be opened without obtaining authorization from you first. If you do become a victim of identity theft, the company will help you to recover. Some companies will also offer insurance up to a specific amount in case you incur losses due to identity theft.

Do your research to see which company is the best fit for you. Here are some to start with: Identity Guard, LifeLock, Experian IdentityWorks, IdentityForce, myFICO, and IDShield.

CHAPTER 24
INFLATION and QUANTITATIVE EASING

<u>Inflation</u>

Inflation occurs when there is a general increase in the price of goods and services, which in turn means that the purchasing power of your money decreases. In other words, with inflation, your dollar will buy less now than it did before. There are a number of causes for inflation. In some cases, inflation is the result of a situation which causes the *price of goods and services to increase*. Other times, inflation is the result of a situation which causes the *value of money to decrease*; that is, money itself becomes worth less rather than goods or services becoming worth more.

Changes in supply and demand are one cause of inflation. Supply and demand affect the price of goods or services. If supply is high (that is, if an item is readily and easily available) and demand is low (an item is not readily and easily available), the price will be lower. If supply is low and demand is high, the price will be higher.

Sometimes, a government will pay for things by printing more money or by electronically creating more money (more on this below). You would think that printing more money may boost the economy; however, in some cases it can have the opposite effect because it causes inflation.

Why is this? Supply and demand come into play. Let's say the government prints money and increases the amount of money in circulation. In this case, it is not the supply of a good or service which has increased; instead, there an increase in the supply of money itself. Say we have 100 cars, each worth $25,000. If the amount of money in circulation increased, there would still be 100 cars, but because people have more money to spend, demand for the cars will increase. Since there is an increased demand for the cars, dealers can raise the price, for example, to $30,000. In this example, since the amount of money in circulation increased, it now takes more money to buy the same car.

Here are a few other examples which can cause inflation:

- There are laws which specify a minimum wage for workers. What happens when the minimum wage is increased? Where do employers get the money to pay for the increase? The increase in cost is passed on to the consumer, so the cost is paid by all of us in the form of higher prices. Increased labor costs in turn increase the cost of products, both because labor is required to secure the raw materials needed to make the products and because labor is required to manufacture the products.
- When the cost to produce fuel increases, the cost of transportation also increases. This includes transporting products and contributes to an increase in the overall price of products, as well.

Governments like inflation. If people earn more money, they pay more in income taxes. If products cost more, more sales tax revenue is generated. This tax money goes to the government.

Inflation in part is controlled by governments and, in the case of the United States and other affiliated nations, The Federal Reserve. When inflation generates more tax money, some of this money can be used to pay off some of the national debt. If the prices of products decrease and less tax money is generated (deflation), it is more difficult to pay off the debt. Some believe the Federal Reserve manipulates the economy regularly, by raising and lowering loan interest rates. Decreased or increased interest rates mean that borrowing money is cheaper or more expensive for the consumer.

Think of inflation as a hidden tax. Back in the 1950s, the average salary of a doctor was $11,000 a year, a fraction of a doctor's salary today; however, the 1950s doctor was able to buy more than a doctor can buy today. In 1950, you could buy a brand-new Volkswagen for around $1,300. As a child in the 1960s, I remember that gasoline cost 27 cents per gallon, and an ice cream cone was five cents. Think about this: We may make more money now than our parents made at our age, but our money is worth less than theirs was!

Quantitative Easing:

Quantitative easing is a fancy way of saying the government "prints more money". The government does not actually print more money; instead, the federal government central bank increases the money supply to consumers. They do this by purchasing long-term financial securities, such as U.S. government bonds. This increases the supply of money on the open market, which is designed to encourage consumers to borrow and invest money.

Let's put into simple terms how quantitative easing hurts all of us by using an example with a savings account. Say I have $100 in my savings account. If the government doubles the money supply today, then my $100 will buy only half of the goods that it could yesterday. In essence, my $100 is now worth only $50. In reality, the money supply does not double overnight. Quantitative easing happens gradually (like the fable where a frog is slowly boiled alive). If change happens gradually, you feel it less.

CHAPTER 25
INVESTMENTS

"You are not rich if you work for your money.
Rich people don't work for their money; their money works for them."
- Unknown

There is some truth to this quote. Most self-made millionaires accumulated wealth by working AND investing their money. Here are a few common things to learn about investing and letting your money work for you.

<u>Money Market Savings</u>

A money market savings account is a basic savings account at your local bank. Interest earned from a money market account is usually guaranteed and has little risk; however, the interest rate is very low, so you earn very little. Currently, the interest rate is less than 1% a year! In some cases, the bank may charge fees. If fees are greater than the amount of interest earned, you may actually lose money, hence the term "negative interest rate". A savings account may be used for your emergency funds, but for any other savings, a low-interest savings account should be used as a temporary holding place for your money until you can invest it, or it can be a place to keep your money between investments. It is important to have funds which are immediately accessible in case of an emergency, but this may be at the expense of earning low or no interest.

Certificates of Deposit

A Certificate of Deposit (CD) pays more interest than a money market account, but you must commit to investing the money for a specified amount of time, such as six months, one year, two years, three years, five years, or more. The greater amount of time you choose, the higher the interest rate you will earn. Currently, the interest rate is between 2% and 5% annually.

Bonds:

Savings Bonds

Issued by the US Government, a savings bond eventually has a worth of its "face" value. You purchase the bond usually for one-half the face value, and then accrue interest based on a rate which is determined at the time the bond is issued (a fixed rate). The bonds mature after a pre-defined number of years, and at that time, the U.S. Treasury will guarantee that you are paid the face value of the bond.

Here is an example: You pay $50 to purchase a $100 savings bond which will mature in 20 years. Depending on the type of bond, it may continue to earn interest for 30 years. This means that at 20 years, the bond is worth face value of $100, and in 30 years, the $100 bond can be worth more than $100. (This is good because, due to inflation, your money is worth less than it was ten years ago!) I have some old savings bonds which were issued 28 years ago. They have managed to earn 4% interest annually, which is better than most savings accounts. They are backed by the "full faith" of the U.S. Government.

Corporate Bonds

Corporate bonds are issued by large companies, usually to finance large projects or company expansion. These bonds are usually held for a year or more and pay interest rates between 4% and 10%. There are two basic types of corporate bonds, high-grade (also called investment-grade) and high-yield (also called non-investment-grade, speculative-grade, or junk bonds). High-grade bonds are usually issued by well-established companies and have a lower risk. High-yield bonds are issued by lesser-established companies and pay a higher interest rate due to the higher risk involved. Interest made on corporate bonds is usually paid out twice a year, and the income is taxable by the government.

Municipal Bonds

Municipal bonds are issued by a state or local government and are used to raise money for major projects such as building bridges, road construction, schools, etc. The risk and interest rate of each bond is based on the financial stability and strength of the issuing municipality. Interest earned is often tax free, meaning you don't have to pay federal and state taxes on the income. The interest rate is usually less than that of corporate bonds, but you need to take into consideration the money saved by not paying taxes. Since you don't pay taxes on earnings from a municipal bond, you may actually earn more money with a municipal bond which pays a lower interest rate than with a corporate bond which pays a higher interest rate. Often, a minimum investment of $5,000 is required, which limits purchase by some buyers.

Annuities

An annuity is purchased from an insurance company and is a long-term investment. You can purchase an annuity either by paying a lump sum or by making payments over a period of time. After a designated time period, the amount you purchased is converted into payments (from the insurance company to you) designed to last throughout your life.

Money in an annuity is invested in a wide range of products which generate different levels of income with different levels of risk. You control how much to contribute, how the money is invested, and the payout amount based on the amount of your contributions.

An advantage to an annuity is that it allows you to save a large amount of money which is tax-deferred, which means you don't pay income taxes on money earned until you withdraw it from the annuity. The benefit to being tax deferred is that you are likely to draw the money from the annuity when you are retired, at a time when you have a lower income and are in a lower tax bracket (and therefore pay less in taxes). 401(k) and IRA retirement accounts are also tax-deferred; however, there is a limit to how much you can put into these accounts each year. Disadvantages to annuities is that fees can be higher than with other investments.

Annuities also act somewhat similar to a life insurance policy. Similar to an insurance policy or bank account, you designate a beneficiary. If you should die before the entire annuity is paid to you, the payments will go to your beneficiary. Some annuities allow you to collect money while you are still alive (whereas a term life insurance policy pays only upon death). The most common annuities are lifetime annuities.

Stock Market

Want to get rich quick? Buy stock. Want to lose all your money overnight? Buy stock.

A stock is a share of ownership in a company or corporation. Let's explain. A company can either be privately owned or publicly owned. A privately-owned company is owned by an individual, a group of individuals, or a corporation. A publicly-owned company is one where part of the company owned by the general public.

When purchasing stock, it means that the public may purchase a piece (or pieces) of a company. These pieces are called shares. Each share represents a percentage of ownership in the company. The corporation will have many shares of stock, and these shares are bought and sold (traded) on a stock exchange or other market. The number of shares available for sale is usually determined by an investment banking company. The investment banking company also determines the initial stock price, known as the Initial Public Offering (IPO).

Let's talk a bit about the terms "stocks" and "shares". In American English, the two words often refer to the same thing. In general, "stock" is used as a more general term, when speaking of owning "pieces" of companies in general, and "share" is used when speaking of owning "pieces" of a specific company. For example, I may say that I own stocks in several companies, and I own 100 shares of Microsoft.

The price of a stock increases if the company is successful and makes more money than it spends, OR if there are a lot of people who speculate that the company will be successful. This speculation will drive up the price of the stock. For example, say Apple announces that the company is introducing a brand-new revolutionary product and expects to sell millions of the product. If public investors speculate that Apple will make a lot of money in the future (even though sales have not yet occurred), this will drive up the cost of a share in the company. On the other hand, if a company does poorly, or if there is an incident which harms the company's reputation, the price of company shares may decrease.

Sometimes the price of a share will increase so much that the cost of a share becomes too high for small investors. To make shares more affordable, the company may "split" the stock. This increases the number of shares available to the public and lowers the price per share. For example, if a company has one million shares with each share worth $100, the company may split the stock so that there are now two million shares, with each share worth $50. The total value remains the same.

There is risk when investing in the stock market. Many people have made a lot of money in the stock market; however, there have also been times when the stock market has done poorly or "crashed", and people lost a lot of money.

There have been a number of stock market crashes throughout history. The most devastating U.S. stock market crash occurred in 1929. This crash led to the "Great Depression", which saw the U.S. economy collapse and unemployment skyrocket. It wasn't until more than a decade later, during World War II, that the U.S. recovered from the 1929 stock market crash (jobs are created during war time, because a work force is needed to manufacture things such as tanks, planes, supplies, and other items).

Another major stock market crashed occurred on "Black Monday" in 1987, and once again people lost much of the money they had invested. More recently, the stock market crashed in 2008, and many people saw their retirement savings vanish overnight. Families lost their homes. As a result of these crashes, some elderly people found themselves back in the work force in their golden years, when they thought they would be retired and taking life easy. Some people had invested too much of their money in stocks. As a result, many lost their retirement nest egg and had to work long past normal retirement age.

Now we'll talk about success stories. Some people become wealthy because they purchase stock in companies such as Apple or Microsoft when the companies are young. We'll use Microsoft as an example of a success story. When Microsoft first sold stock in 1986, the cost was $21 a share. Microsoft stock has since split nine times, so a share purchased at the beginning (and never sold) would now be 512 shares. In May of 2017, the Microsoft share price was $68; this means that if you had purchased one share for $21 in 1986, it would have grown to $34,816 in 2017!! If you had invested $2,100 to purchase 100 shares in 1986, the stock would have been worth more than $3.4 million dollars in 2017!!

Unfortunately, for every success story there are hundreds of failures and losses. If you hear about the next company to make huge gains like Microsoft, Amazon, or Netflix, let us know!

Dividends

When public companies make money, profits are distributed to the shareholders. Dividends are the earnings paid to the shareholders. There are two main types of dividends, cash dividends and stock dividends, where a shareholder is paid either in cash or with additional shares of stock. Cash dividends are the most common and are usually paid by well-established companies who don't need the cash in order to grow the company. Companies which are growing or are newly established need the cash for expansion, so they are more likely to pay dividends as additional shares of stock.

Stock Market Index

People who invest in the stock market need a way to monitor the market, compare activity on various investments, and determine a market's return on investment. A stock market index, or stock index, is used for this purpose. It is calculated by using prices of selected stocks.

A stock index reflects the prices and values of large companies, to help track how these groups of companies are doing as a whole. You may hear in the news how the Dow Industrials went up or down so many points. This means that the total value of the companies in the index increased or decreased by a certain percentage (points or basis points are equal to one hundredth of a percent, or 0.01%. So, an increase in 500 basis points means that the value increased by 0.5%). As mentioned earlier, stock prices are not set by the intrinsic value of the company (which would be hard to determine). Rather, they are set by the amount people are willing to buy and sell the stock shares for. Often, individual investors cannot set the price of a stock (unless you're selling directly to a friend); rather, these prices are determined by large mutual funds or institutional investors, which trade stock on places such as the New York Stock Exchange.

In general, when people sell stock in companies that make up an index, the index number tends to go down. This is because when a stock is sold, it is sold for less than the purchase price of a stock. When people buy stock in companies that make up an index, the index number goes up because the purchase price is higher than the selling price. The index goes up when people buy because they put money into the system. When they sell, they take money out of the system, causing the index to go down.

There are many stock indices. Here are some of the most common:

Dow Jones Industrial Average:
Also known as "The Dow". This index tracks 30 large United States companies.

Standard and Poor's 500:
Also known as the "S&P". This index tracks 500 large United States companies.

National Association of Securities Dealers Automated Quotations System:
Also known as NASDAQ. An American stock exchange, it is second in size only to the New York stock exchange. Several technology companies are traded on the NASDAQ.

Price-to-Earnings Ratio

The price-to-earnings ratio (PE Ratio) is the current market price of a share divided by the earnings per share.

$$P / E \text{ Ratio} = \frac{\text{Market value per share}}{\text{Earnings per share}}$$

If a PE Ratio is high (more than 16:1), this could mean two things; one, that a company's stock is over-valued, or two, that investors anticipate that earnings will grow in the future. If earnings are expected to grow in the future, investors are willing to pay more for a share even though the company does not currently generate earnings to justify the price. When purchasing a stock with a high PE Ratio, you take a risk, but it indicates that other investors also have faith in the company's potential for future earnings (or they are all equally wrong!).

Mutual Funds

A mutual fund is a group of stocks (an investment fund) which pools money from many investors to purchase the stocks. The fund is managed by an investment company in order to reduce risk and/or maximize the amount of money the fund will make. It is managed by investment professionals who buy and sell stocks to maximize performance and/or minimize risk. There are hundreds of mutual funds, each with a different focus, mix, and balance of companies. Funds may have a specific emphasis on certain areas with focus on such things as technology, healthcare, or defense contracts. A mutual fund may also have a wide variation in its risk and return. A high-risk fund typically has a higher rate of return; however, it also has a higher risk of loss. Risk is determined by the volatility of the company, industry, or product that the company deals in. Risk is also determined by speculation as to how much the company is expected to earn or create.

Chapter 26
Other Investment Opportunities

<u>Real Estate</u>

When you purchase a home and the value of the home increases, your owner's equity in the home increases, as well. The equity is the difference between the value of the home and how much you owe on the home loan. For example, if your home is worth $600,000, and you owe $200,000 on the home loan, then you have $400,000 in equity. That is, you would receive $400,000 if you sold the home for $600,000.

So, if you purchase a home and the value of the home increases, you can sell the home and make money. Many people make money by buying a home which needs a lot of work (a "fixer upper"), repairing and renovating the home, and then selling it for a profit. (This is known as "flipping".) If you purchase a home in a neighborhood which has a high demand for homes, AND property values increase, you can make a lot of money. If you purchase a home and the value of surrounding homes increase, the value of your home will also increase, whether you fix it up or not.

On the other hand, remember "underwater mortgages" discussed in Chapter 8. If the value of the home decreases, then you may lose money. Timing is everything. We can't predict the future; we can only make educated decisions. The more knowledge we have, the better financial decisions we can make.

Another real estate option is to purchase property and rent it out. Once you pay the monthly loan payment and budget all your expenses, any rental income that exceeds your costs becomes profit. This is how people turn real estate into regular income. Even if the rent you receive only covers the mortgage payment and other expenses, you will make money when you sell the property, if the property value increases after you purchase the property. That is, you can build equity over the years, which turns into cash when you sell the property.

Now that you know how to create a budget, you can do the math and determine whether or not you can invest in real estate. Remember, the biggest problems for most people is coming up with enough money for a down payment and qualifying for a loan based on their credit rating.

One way to fund a down payment is to obtain a home equity line of credit (also known as a "second mortgage") on your existing home. However, if you do this, you had better be sure the idea will work. Know the risks. If you don't have a good tenant, if the property value decreases, or you cannot pay your monthly loan payments, you run the risk of losing both properties (your home and the rental property). If it does work out, you will receive a regular monthly income. If the property does not require a lot of regular maintenance, it can be a very profitable investment with a minimal amount of work. It is an example of your letting your money work for you.

Precious Metals

Owning gold, silver, platinum, and some other precious metals can sometimes be used as a hedge, or protection, from inflation or economic fluctuations. Precious metal values are based on the markets; that is, prices are affected by the laws of supply and demand.

Some investors have precious metals in their investment portfolios. Some do not consider the purchase of precious metals really as an investment, but instead as a way to preserve wealth. An analogy is that in ancient Roman times, an ounce of gold might be used to buy a nice suit and a pair of shoes (well, maybe a nice toga and sandals). The same can be said today.

The monetary value of an ounce of gold may vary considerably because the value of the dollar varies. Another factor is demand. For instance, if people fear that the value of the dollar is going decrease (become worth less, or maybe "worthless"), and they buy gold as a hedge, then this will drive up the price of gold. Supply and demand.

The value of silver and platinum also vary, but these precious metals also have industrial uses, which make them valuable in other ways. Historically, gold does not have as many industrial uses as silver or platinum, but it has value because it is scarcer. It also has more beauty and has had a higher perceived value (we want it) since ancient times, versus intrinsic value (we need it). Silver trades at a lower price than gold and therefore is more affordable and within reach financially for the average person. At the time of this writing, gold was valued at more than $1,600 per ounce, which is not within the reach of everyone.

Gold is often traded in gold coins, each typically weighing one ounce. There are also coins weighing half-ounce, quarter ounce, and 1/10-ounce coins, which help to make gold ownership more affordable. The cost of platinum is also high and is close to the cost of gold, sometimes higher, sometimes lower. At the time of this writing, silver is trading at around $15 per ounce, and platinum at around $750 per ounce.

Silver is also purchased by survivalists, as it can be used to trade for low-cost items during times of uncertainty. For example, if the economy of a country collapsed, its currency may be worth nothing, but you could purchase gasoline for your car and pay for it with an ounce or two of silver. Think how difficult it would be to make change for a tank of gas if you paid with an ounce of gold.

Important note if you plan on purchasing gold, silver, or platinum as an investment: When you sell a capital asset at a profit, the profit is called a "capital gain". This is income, so you must pay income taxes; however, precious metals are categorized as "collectibles". Taxes on collectibles are handled differently than taxes on other assets.

Normally, if you own a capital asset for one year or less before selling, the income is called a "short-term capital gain"; if owned longer than one year, the income is a "long-term" capital gain. In most cases, short-term capital gains are taxed at a higher rate than long-term capital gains; that is, you pay a higher tax if you own an asset for one year or less.

In the case of collectibles, if you sell the assets at a profit at one year or less, the profit is considered normal income and taxed at your normal income tax rate, which is usually higher than the short-term capital gains tax rate. In addition, if you sell and make a profit after owning the assets for more than one year, capital gains on collectibles are taxed at the short-term capital gains tax rate (around 28%) instead of the long-term capital gains rate (around 15%). So, you will pay higher taxes on profits made from the sale of precious metals than you would for other assets. In my opinion, this is the government's way of discouraging investing in precious metals, because the government has less control over precious metals versus the dollar.

Cryptocurrency

Cryptocurrency is an internet-based electronic monetary system. It is a medium used to exchange value from all over the world. Instead of a physical object such as a coin or paper currency, cryptocurrency is digital and use encryption techniques to control money and transfer funds. Blockchain is the technology which enables cryptocurrency to function. Bitcoin was the first cryptocurrency, developed in 2008 by an unknown inventor "named" Satoshi Nakamoto. There are now a number of cryptocurrencies, but Bitcoin is still the most prominent.

Since its beginning in 2008, Bitcoin has increased tremendously in value. Some governments, including the U.S., do not recognize cryptocurrency as a "currency". Instead, they designate it as "property. At the time of its creation, one Bitcoin was worth less than one cent. Today, one Bitcoin is worth thousands of dollars. Those who had purchased a lot of Bitcoin early on and held on to it are now multi-millionaires.

Blockchain technology uses an encrypted computer ledger which lists all Bitcoin transactions. There are computers worldwide which have a copy of the same ledger, and the cryptocurrency transactions are copied to these ledgers. The ledger is decentralized and is not under the control of any one person or country. It is also highly encrypted and supposedly unhackable. There are multiple copies of the ledger which are all the same, in order to maintain integrity and prevent centralized control. Bitcoin is not backed by gold or by silver or by any government. It has value as a medium of exchange and as a store of wealth. It has no intrinsic value per se; its value is that it can securely store wealth.

Bitcoin is created by a process known as "mining". By design, there will be a limit of 21 million Bitcoin created by the mining process. Unlike a government-created currency, once the 21 million Bitcoins are released, there will be no additional Bitcoin created. Sometimes when governments run out of money, they just print or release more money into the community. The more they print, the less your saved currency is worth. Once the 21 million Bitcoin are released, a Bitcoin may be purchased only from an existing owner, at ever increasing prices. When more people buy cryptocurrency, prices are driven upward. Supply and demand.

Bitcoin is created by the mining process. Mining is done by banks of computers which work to solve complex mathematical problems. The first group of computers to solve the mathematical problem is rewarded with a certain number of Bitcoins. As time goes on, the number of Bitcoins given as a reward will decrease until all 21 million are released. The last Bitcoin is expected to be released around the year 2038. A miner which solves a problem creates a file (or a "block") which contains all recent Bitcoin transactions, and the file is "chained" to the previous block; hence, the term "blockchain". Since the Bitcoin mining process consumes a vast amount of electricity to operate the computers, there is a high cost in electrical power to create one Bitcoin. Cryptocurrency is not created out of thin air for free; therefore, a single bitcoin represents, at a minimum, the electrical energy necessary for its creation.

As economies and banks fail worldwide, the people of these nations are purchasing Bitcoin as a way to preserve their wealth. Sound familiar? People from countries such as China, India, and Venezuela have purchased Bitcoin as their money became devalued or worthless. It's no wonder Bitcoin has been referred to as "Cyber Gold".

Cryptocurrency is bought and sold via the internet. All you need to conduct transactions is a computer or other electronic device. This process has the potential to bring banking to millions of people in third world countries who currently don't have access to banking. You can see that the banking system can feel threatened, as increased use of cryptocurrency may make some banking transactions obsolete. Buying and selling a cryptocurrency is usually done through an internet-based cryptocurrency "exchange" company. When using these exchanges to buy or sell cryptocurrency anywhere in the world, you may use your local currency to transfer your money between the exchange and your bank.

Bitcoin can also be used to pay for goods and services. The number of businesses which accept Bitcoin increases on a daily basis. There are Bitcoin ATMs where you may buy Bitcoin or sell your Bitcoin for the local currency. Japan recognizes Bitcoin as a legitimate currency and regulates it for the protection of the buyers. Bitcoin is also now accepted in Japan by major businesses, and the number of businesses is growing daily. Other countries are following Japan's example.

On the other hand, some countries are making cryptocurrencies illegal. Existing fiat currency (money which is not backed by gold or other physical commodity) and conventional banking systems can be manipulated by governments and the ultra-wealthy, which control the existing Federal Reserve System and its international equivalents. (The Federal Reserve is privately run and is no more Federal than Federal Express is!) Alternative financial vehicles such as cryptocurrency threaten current banking systems and the status quo.

As a result of Bitcoin's rapid growth, Bitcoin has found some inadequacies in the blockchain technology. Other cryptocurrencies have learned from Bitcoin's experience and corrected some of these inadequacies in their own blockchain technologies. For example, newer blockchains boast much faster transaction times and lower fees, and they can also provide other functions such as smart contracts. A smart contract is like an automatic electronic escrow which holds funds between two parties until a task is completed.

Each cryptocurrency has its own niche. Some offer complete privacy and anonymity. Some, such as Ripple and Cardano, were designed to provide better electronic transmission of financial transactions, and they threaten existing systems like SWIFT and VISA. Others, such as Ethereum, are adaptable to a number of applications. There are hundreds of other cryptocurrencies known as "Altcoins" (short for alternative coin), and new cryptocurrencies are created as time goes on. One major difference between Altcoins and Bitcoin is that companies and individuals control Altcoins. No one person or company has control of Bitcoin. This is the unique value and strength of Bitcoin. Governments can try to regulate and even outlaw Bitcoin, but it is impossible for them to stop or confiscate Bitcoin.

The potential applications for blockchain technology are almost limitless; it can be used for everything from identity verification to securing medical records to transferring money and financial data. Banks are looking into blockchain technology to replace international money transfer systems like SWIFT, and some countries are looking into developing their own cyber currency, based on blockchain technology. Paper money is fast becoming obsolete. Blockchain technology is currently in its infancy, so expect big growth, technology changes, and breakthroughs in the near future.

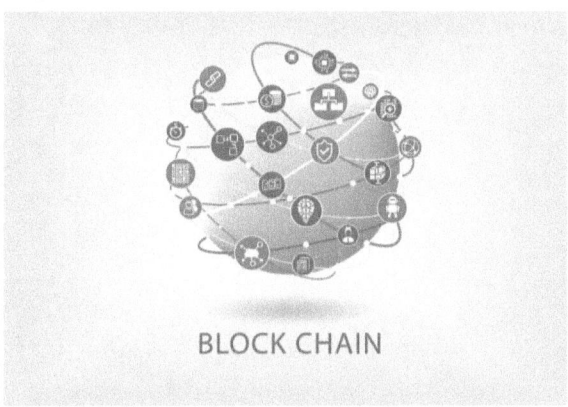

BLOCK CHAIN

Some countries are jumping on the cryptocurrency bandwagon by offering their own cryptocurrencies. If you think about it; the American dollar exists almost completely in cyberspace. Credit card charges are transmitted electronically. Banking transactions are done electronically. Paper currency is fast becoming obsolete and is being replaced by electronic-based technology such as Apple Pay, Venmo, Zelle, or Pay Pal. The key here is that these systems are still based on the dollar, which is controlled by the US government and the Federal Reserve system. The dollar is manipulated at will to suit the government's interests, the interests of banks, and the interests of individuals who control the Federal Reserve system. Governments have the ability to create more currency by printing more. Not so with Bitcoin, which has a finite amount of 21 million units. Bitcoin is not controlled by a single government, company or individual. Governments cannot destroy Bitcoin. Here lies Bitcoin's real value.

Although gains by investing in cryptocurrency can be very attractive, remember that all investments have risk. With cryptocurrencies, the risk can be substantial. Do not invest in cryptocurrencies unless you can afford to lose the money. Don't go into debt to buy cryptocurrency, and don't buy cryptocurrency if you owe a lot of money on things like credit cards. Those debts need to be paid first. Cryptocurrencies have huge value swings. There have been people who incurred debt so that they could purchase cryptocurrency at high prices, only to see prices later fall, and then were frantic when seeing their losses. Some obtained credit card cash advances or took out second mortgages on their houses to buy cryptocurrency during upswings, but then were unable to survive downswings because they leveraged their purchases; they did not earn enough gains to cover the minimum payments on their purchases.

Keep in mind, just as with stocks, you don't actually gain or lose until you sell. If there is a case where value is lost because prices decreased after purchasing cryptocurrency, those who can hold on for dear life (HODL) until prices rise again don't have to worry about the fear of missing out (FOMO). Interesting how these two positions have their own acronyms!

Chapter 27
Taxes

It is said that the only sure things in life are death and taxes. The average person pays dozens of taxes. You don't think so? Every time you buy gasoline, you pay a federal tax, and often a state tax. When you purchase something, there is usually a sales tax. Telephone and utility bills have various taxes included. If a family member dies and leaves money to you, the government has even figured out a way to tax DEAD people by charging an estate tax! Remember that the family member who died already paid an income tax on that money, so the government has double or even triple taxed the money by the time you receive it. For the sake of simplicity, in this book we will focus on the big taxes.

"We made $30,000 more last year
and it only cost us $60,000."

(Making more money may put you in a higher tax bracket in which you will pay more in taxes)

Federal income tax is a tax on the money you earn, that is, your income. It is a tax imposed by the federal government. For many people, this is their largest tax. Tax rates range between 10% and 37%. This means that 10 to 37 cents of every dollar you earn goes to the United States Federal Government. In general, the more money you make, the higher tax rate (percentage in your income that you pay in taxes) you will pay. Federal income tax is collected by the Internal Revenue Service (IRS).

Most employers deduct income taxes from your paycheck. A percentage is taken from each paycheck so that your income taxes are paid throughout the year. The amount deducted is determined by various factors, including the amount of money you make, how many dependents you have (or claim), and what state you live in. If you are a parent with a stay-at-home spouse and two children, you have three dependents, or four if you want to count yourself.

When claiming dependents, you may claim the actual number of dependents or fewer, than the actual number. There are advantages and disadvantages to both. For example, if you have four dependents and claim all four, you will have a certain dollar amount deducted from each paycheck. When annual income taxes are due and you find that you owe more than what was deducted from your paycheck, you may want to go to your employer and change your number of dependents to two or three. This will result in a higher deduction from each paycheck. That is, more money will be held from each paycheck so that you won't end up owing more money at tax time, or you may even receive a tax refund after you file your taxes.

Some people like to claim fewer dependents so they will receive a big refund each year. The advantage to this is that every year you will receive a lump sum, to save or spend as you wish. The disadvantage is that the government has your money during the year, whereas you could have invested the money if you had it. Many people have a tendency to spend the money when they receive their paycheck, rather than save or invest, so receiving a tax refund each year may be a better option. Saving and investing takes discipline, desire, and education.

What you don't want to do is claim more dependents than you actually have. This can result in too little being deducted from your paycheck, which means you may owe a lot of money (money that you may longer have!) when taxes are due each year, and you will have to pay a penalty if you cannot pay the amount you owe on time. If you claim more dependents than you actually have in order to pay less in taxes, this is fraud and is punishable by law, so don't do it!

State Income Tax

State income tax is also a tax on your income; however, this tax is imposed by the state you live or work in, rather than the federal government. Some states do not charge a state income tax, such as Alaska, Florida, Texas, South Dakota, Washington, Wyoming and Nevada,. Some state income tax rates are as low as 3% (Pennsylvania) or as high as 13% (California). (This is one reason why many retirees leave California upon retirement.)

Income Tax Deductions

A tax deduction is a deduction from your income, which in turn lowers the amount you must pay in income taxes. Certain expenses or donations qualify as tax deductions. If you have a qualifying expense or donation, you may subtract a certain amount from your income.

Some examples of allowable tax deductions are charitable contributions, business expenses, medical expenses, work-related education expenses, interest on home loans, and property taxes. There are more; you can find additional information from your tax preparer or tax-preparation software.

Here's an example. Let's say you make $50,000 a year. You donated $2,000 to the church and had $3,000 in qualifying expenses for your home business, for a total of $5,000 in tax deductions. This means you pay taxes on $45,000 instead of $50,000. If you are in the 25% tax bracket, this means you would pay $11,250 in taxes (25% of $45,000) instead of $12,500 (25% of 50,000), for a savings of $1,250. There are many rules associated with tax deductions, so you must learn which rules apply to the deductions you wish to use. This is a simplified explanation to give you the general idea as to what an income tax deduction is all about.

The above example is an example of "itemized" deductions, where you list all the expenses or donations which qualify as tax deductions (that is, you list each item, or "itemize"). Another type of tax deduction is the "standard" deduction. The standard deduction is a fixed amount which is determined by the government, based on how much money you make, whether you are married and filing jointly, and how many dependents you have.

For some people, their itemized deductions may have a higher dollar amount than the standard deduction. For these people, they are better off itemizing their deductions and using this amount to lower their taxable income. For those who do not have enough expenses or donations which qualify for tax deductions, the standard deduction may be higher. When completing your income tax forms, you choose the deduction that is the higher of the two (standard or itemized). In general, people that have their own business (sole proprietor) will do better itemizing deductions, especially if the business is successful.

It is important that you keep track of any expenses you may deduct by listing them in a ledger, spreadsheet, or financial computer program such as Quicken or QuickBooks. You would be surprised how a few dollars here or there over the course of a year can total to over a few thousand dollars. If you paid more taxes than you owe, then you may receive a refund from your state and/or federal government, after you file your tax returns.

<u>Filing Income Taxes</u>

Income taxes must be "filed", meaning you must complete and submit the appropriate tax forms for each government entity (federal and state) by a deadline, usually by April 15th of each year. Separate forms are used for federal and state governments. You may hire an accountant, or you may complete the forms yourself.

There are computer software programs available, such as TurboTax or LibertyTax, which are a tremendous aid in completing income tax forms; they make it easy. The computer program will ask a series of questions and then complete the form for you based on your answers. The software can analyze your information and help you to maximize your deductions, resulting in a higher refund or a reduction in the amount of taxes you must pay. You have the option to submit your tax forms to the government electronically or by mail. It will also calculate the likelihood of an IRS audit (likened to a financial rectal exam). The average price for a basic software program is around $60. You may pay more for a more complex program if your tax situation is more complex, but it is well worth it. Another advantage to using a computer program is that it keeps track of your information from prior years; this makes filing taxes easier in subsequent years.

Self-Employment and Contract Labor

"I hear you have a side business."

A person who is self-employed is one that is not an employee of another person or company. Instead, they own their own business or work as a freelancer. A self-employed person may perform work for someone else in the form of a contract; hence, the terms "contractor" or "contract laborer".

The reason it is important to cover this labor distinction in a finance book is that income taxes are handled differently. Normally, an employer is required to deduct money from your paychecks to pay income taxes. If you are self-employed, you are responsible to make sure that you have enough money to pay your income taxes each year.

A self-employed person or contractor must register their business with the government and obtain an Employer Identification Number (EIN), also known as a Federal Tax Identification Number (FEIN or Tax ID Number). If a contractor works with a large company, the contractor may have to provide their Tax ID Number to the company so that the company may provide tax information to you and to the government, and so that you may receive a 1099 Tax Form.

If you are a permanent or regular employee employed by an employer, you will receive a W-2 form each year, which contains information about the income and payroll taxes withheld from your paycheck. For contract workers, businesses will provide a 1099 form instead. The 1099 form states the contractor's earnings for the year, who paid those earnings, and other tax information. Businesses don't withhold or pay taxes on the behalf of a contract worker, so a 1099 does not include this information. If you are a contractor who performs work for several businesses, you will receive a 1099 from each business.

If you do not receive a 1099 form from a business from which you earned money, you are still responsible to pay taxes on the income earned. It is important to keep good records on your income and pay taxes on all income received. Also, keep good records and receipts for all expenses associated with your business, as they may be eligible for tax deductions.

If you are a contract laborer, it is important that you put aside money each month so that you may pay your income taxes each year (often paid quarterly). You will need to estimate how much income you will generate and what tax rate (tax bracket) that will put you in, so that you may plan and save accordingly. The tax bracket is determined by your income. Those who have a lower income pay a smaller percentage in taxes, and those who have a higher income pay a higher percentage in taxes. You can find the information for each bracket online. Note that some states do not have income taxes; however, just about everyone must pay federal income taxes.

Let's look at an example. To keep it simple, we will include only income and not deductions. Say you earned $10,000 for the year and are in the 12% federal tax bracket. This means you will owe $1,200 to the IRS for federal income taxes that year. In your state, your $10,000 income puts you into the 7% tax bracket. This means you will owe $700 in state income taxes. So, you will need a total of $1,900 to pay your taxes. What if you made $50,000? This would put you in the 22% bracket and you would need $11,000 to pay the federal and state income taxes. And if you made $100,000? You would be in the 24% bracket and you would pay $24,000 in taxes. (Remember, you can reduce the amount owed in taxes by using appropriate tax deductions).

So, you can see the importance for self-employed people to plan ahead and save enough to pay income taxes. It is all too common for self-employed people to forget this and spend all their income on other items, and then find themselves in trouble at tax time.

Here are a few things to remember so that you don't find yourself in an income-tax financial trap:

1. Estimate (as best you can) your income for the year.
2. Add this to all other sources of taxable income to find the total income. (Not all income is taxable. For example, money earned in most retirement accounts are not taxable until money is withdrawn)
3. Keep track of all business-related expenses but remember that not all business-related expenses are tax deductible.
4. Research the federal and state tax brackets for the given year to determine which tax bracket you belong to.
5. Remember also that you may pay other fees and taxes, such as Social Security and State Disability.
6. Do your research. On-line programs are available to those who are self-employed, which provide tax calculators, automated withholding on 1099 income, expense itemizations, and quarterly IRS filings.
7. Determine your estimated taxes and put this into your budget. After doing your research to determine the best fit for you, put a mechanism into place to pay your taxes on a regular basis (often quarterly).
8. Continue to track your income and expenses each month. You may need to make adjustments throughout the year, as your income increases or decreases from your original estimate.
9. Remember to keep to your budget, allowing for savings and retirement account contributions.

If you are self-employed and do these steps, you will be in better financial shape. If you ignore the need to save and pay your income taxes, you can be assured that you will pay penalties and interest. Never pay more money than you have to, so make your tax payments on time and in the correct amounts!

"There is no getting away from you guys."

The IRS audits a small percentage of the American public every year. The chance of an audit increases if you don't follow the rules or if you try to take advantage of the tax system by deducting more than you should.

It's been said that a dreaded audit by the IRS is similar to getting a colonoscopy. You don't want strangers looking at your personal finances any more than you want them looking up your anal orifices! An IRS audit is an invasion of your financial privacy, and one that is not optional if you are selected for an audit. It means digging up your financial records for as long as the last seven years (if you can find them!) and having every financial decision you make come under scrutiny by an IRS auditor.

One of the most basic ways to avoid an audit is to use common sense: File your taxes properly and on time. Don't think that if you don't file your income taxes, the taxes will just go away. Once you are in the IRS system through an employer or by filing taxes for the first time, you are forever on their radar. Even when you die, the government will want to tax your estate. As stated before, we can't avoid death and taxes. No one mentions that the IRS can tax you beyond the grave!

"We've always needed an accounting magician."

You increase your chances for an IRS audit if you have too many deductions with a high dollar amount, such as a large amount of charitable donations or business expenses. If you donate money or goods to any organization, make sure to obtain a receipt and file it away. The IRS requires that you retain financial records and receipts or documentation which support your deductions for seven years.

For example, if you deduct thousands of dollars for a new wardrobe and say that you need it for work, this may flag an IRS audit. The IRS has computerized programs which determine the average acceptable deduction based on your income, type of business, and where you live. If you exceed these averages, you will increase your chance for an audit. The greater the deviation, the higher your name will appear on the audit candidate list. Don't think it is too much trouble for the IRS. They have computers and algorithms that do the work for them. Lists are automatically generated with names for potential audits.

Many self-employed individuals have a lot of business expenses and wish to deduct all of these expenses (rightfully so). However, the deductions must match the income level and be in line with the average deductions of others with a similar business. The general rule is that for every five years of business, your business should show a profit for at least three of the five years. Some home business owners purchase items for the home in the name of the "business" and then repeatedly claim a loss in the business by claiming deductions which exceed their annual income. This may cause the IRS to categorize your business as a "hobby" instead of a "business". A real business exists to make a profit, not create deductions and "cheat" the IRS out of taxes. If you have a home office, you may deduct a percentage of your home expenses such as the mortgage, insurance, and utilities, but there are rules regarding the square footage of the business space in the home and the percentage of time that space is used for business. For example, if your home is 1000 square feet with a 100-square-foot home office, the office space is 10% of the total square footage. IF the office is used exclusively for the home business, you may be able to deduct 10% of your home mortgage, insurance, and utilities as a home office expense. If you use the office space only half of the time for business, then your deduction is 5%. If you deduct more, you may trigger an audit. Again, it is important to know and follow the IRS rules, which may change from year to year.

Business expenses for meals and entertainment also come under scrutiny. It is common for friends to go out for dinner, talk about business for one minute and say, "Ok, we discussed business; this meal will be considered a business expense". If you deduct every meal, season tickets to your favorite sports team, and the Broadway shows you attend, you increase your chances of triggering an audit. Over the years, the IRS has gotten wise to this practice, and meals and entertainment are now deductible at a lower percentage rate than they once were.

The best advice is to be honest. If you attempt to cheat the IRS out of taxes, there is a good chance they will find out. The greater the amount of deductions compared to your income, the higher your chances of receiving a "financial colonoscopy". Leave the colonoscopy to the doctor, not the IRS!

Property Taxes

The next largest tax for many is property tax. This is a tax paid when you own a home or other property. The tax amount is usually 1% to 1.5% of the total value of the property. The tax bill is sent by the local county where the property exists, and often is paid in two installments. In California, the first payment is due in

November and the second payment in February, but there is a "grace period", where payments are not considered late if received by the grace-period deadline. If a payment is received after the grace period deadline, it is considered late and will be assessed a penalty fee.

If your house is worth $500,000, the annual property tax is normally in the area of $5,000 to $7,000, depending on the state and county you live in. That is a lot of money! It is therefore critical that you figure the cost of property taxes before you purchase a home or other property. You might be able to afford the mortgage payment, but can you afford the additional $500 or more per month for the property tax? The county will periodically re-assess property values. If the county determines that your house has increased in value to $600,000, this means the property tax may also increase by $1,000 a year! On rare occasions, the county may find that property values have decreased, in which case your property tax will also decrease. The important thing is to know that property taxes exist, and you must figure the cost into your budget before purchasing property.

Chapter 28
Retirement

I remember when I started working at the hospital where I worked for many years. I was offered the opportunity to participate in the retirement plan. I thought, "heck no, I'm young and will only be working here a few years". Well…almost 30 years later, I was still there. I'm glad that after working eight years, I decided that I had better sign up for the retirement plan.

<u>Early Retirement - A Goal Worth Saving For!</u>

At the hospital, I had a coworker, James, who talked often during his last five years of working about how he could not wait to retire. James told stories about his youth, when he worked his tail off for years as a union employee in a paper mill. After that, he worked for many years at the hospital as a laboratory clerk. James would say, "Man, when I retire, I got it all figured out. We'll sell our home in California and pay cash for a house in Arizona. With the extra money we make from the sale of the (California) house, we are going to spoil our grandkids and really live the life!". James' coworkers heard that story many times. He did exactly what he said he would do. James retired. He and his wife sold their home in Southern California, and they moved to Phoenix, where they purchased their dream house. Sadly, James lived retirement life he had always dreamed of for only six months, when he died suddenly from a massive heart attack.

Another example of people who did not get to enjoy retirement is my parents' story. My father died at the age of 43 from cancer. At the age of 63, my mother became physically disabled and could no longer travel. She lived until the ripe old age of 88 but was never able to enjoy the retirement dream she had hoped and worked for.

We have a number of other similar stories, where family members and friends did not have the chance to enjoy their retirement years. There are also those who slave over a job which they hate and wish they could retire and enjoy life. Due to these reasons, my wife and I decided that we would make our best effort to retire early and enjoy our retirement for as long as we are able. It is not the person who dies with the most toys or the most money that wins. The true winners are those that can enjoy life.

To have the ability to retire and enjoy the retirement life, you must plan and prepare. The perfect life would be to do everything you always wanted to do, go every place you want to go, cross everything off your bucket list, and then spend your last dollar and die of old age. Unfortunately, most of us have no clue how long we are going to live. All we can do is make an educated guess. (A "bucket list" is a list of all the things you want to do before you die. A slang term for dying is to "kick the bucket", hence the saying "bucket list".)

The earlier you retire, the more time you have to enjoy life without the stresses associated with working. Doesn't a 20-or-30-year vacation sound like fun?! It is about quality AND quantity of life. If you retire early, the chances that you can have both increases. Retiring early IS possible if you plan and act accordingly. Your goals can be to spend time with family or friends, travel, do volunteer work, enjoy hobbies, relax, do things for yourself and for the health and sanity of you and your family, or anything else you may you want to do.

"This is where I'm thinking
of putting my husband."

Here is an example of a success story. I have a friend who lives in Alaska. When he was young, he traveled to Los Angeles in an attempt to make it in Hollywood.

We got to be good friends. He reminded me of Peter Frampton and even had the same hair and good looks. Well, Hollywood did not work out the way he had planned, so he went back to Alaska and worked in the oil fields on the Alaskan tundra. He worked hard, installing huge rubber mats in freezing weather on the fragile tundra. The mats were to protect the tundra from heavy equipment and oil derricks. The owner of the company wanted to retire and offered my friend a percentage of company ownership. My friend accepted the offer and eventually ended up owning all of the company, which he sold later for several million dollars, allowing him to retire when he was in his late forties. He has a beautiful wife and three great kids AND is financially secure. He is now in his fifties, healthy, and living a good life in retirement. He continues to manage his money well and is active, travels, enjoys his hobby restoring muscle cars, and invests in property to supplement his retirement income. Remember how we mentioned that the rich often don't work for their money but instead make their money work for them? Well, his money is working for him. His job now is to manage his money and investments, which gives him and his family the time and money to enjoy a quality life together. My friend was lucky in that he was at the right place at the right time, but it was HARD work that ultimately paid off for him and his family. He was one of our inspirations to retire early.

If you plan early, save money, and live within your means, you too can retire early. It takes discipline and sacrifice, but the payday is worth it. There are too many stories of those who work hard so that they may make a living, take an occasional vacation, and eventually retire, only to be disabled or die before or shortly after retiring. Not my idea of a quality life for myself or my family. Remember the song "Cats in the Cradle"? It is a song about a father who was too busy to spend time with his son. The son grew up and did the same thing. He was too busy to spend time with his own family or his aging father. The song is about a cycle of life and death repeating itself, with the family missing out on happiness and quality of life. Spend time with your family, work hard, plan and prepare for expenses and for retirement, and break the cycle!

What Can I Do Now to Prepare for Early Retirement?

When I told my co-workers that I was going to retire, several asked if I had won the lottery! How can a guy, not even 55 years old, who is living in Southern California where the costs of living and healthcare are sky high, retire early? The answer: Plan, save, and live frugally.

When I was 25 years old and working at the hospital, I thought that I did not need to think about retirement because I was so young! Well, I was still working at the hospital after eight years, so I said to myself I had better participate in the retirement plan "just in case". At that age, I thought I would die young just as my father had, so what was the point of saving for retirement? Well…just in case…I decided to participate in the pension plan.

When young, you can better afford to have higher-risk investments such as stocks. As I mentioned previously, investing in higher-risk investments means there is a higher risk that you will make money but also that you may lose money. If you lose money at a young age, you have time to recover from the loss. In most cases, if you invest in a diversified portfolio (investing in a variety of assets) over a long period of time, it is likely that your investment will grow. Remember the chart in Chapter 11, which shows that over time, investment dollars rise and drop, but over time most will rise overall. When you invest, the goal is to make money and then use that money to make even more money. The more you have, the more you can make. The earlier you start, the more time the money has to grow, and it has the capability to grow a lot! Remember to invest wisely. If you invest in high-risk, high-yield investments, only put at risk what you can afford to lose without creating a disastrous financial situation.

Contribute as much to your retirement plan as you can afford, but make sure you are still able to pay all your bills and expenses (both current and future). If circumstances change, you can always revise the amount you contribute to your retirement plan. For instance, the birth of a child may mean higher expenses, so you may need to lower your retirement contributions. On the other hand, if you receive a raise or get a higher-paying job, you may want to increase your retirement contributions.

An important factor if you want to retire early is to live frugally and within your means. If you spend all that you make, then you save nothing. If you save nothing, there is nothing to grow. Hence, you will have little when you retire, except possibly Social Security (or maybe Social Insecurity). If this is the only income you have, you will live at the poverty level. Poverty sucks! If you go into debt, then your situation is even more dire. I am not saying that you can't ever treat yourself, such as going on vacation or buying a nicer car, BUT budget and save for it, as well as for your retirement. You can often afford small luxuries within reason, if you budget and save for them instead of incurring debt. Be patient and plan for your purchases.

Planning is crucial. I don't know of anyone under the age of 35 who is already planning for retirement (other than the character Michael J. Fox played in the 1970's television show Family Ties). If you start saving for your retirement as early as possible, those extra years of saving could mean the difference between retiring young or retiring AFTER normal retirement age.

At first, I did not want to contribute to my employer's retirement plan because there are large penalties if withdraw money from the plan before retirement age. I thought, "What if I die young? Then that money is wasted. I could have been spending and enjoying the money". The key is balance. Spend enough to enjoy your life but make a financial plan just in case you do make it to a ripe old age. Hope for the best but prepare for the worst (I guess getting old is not really the worst).

Depending on the type of account, contributions to your retirement account are often tax deferred. Let's explain. Usually, you must pay an income tax on money earned. If you put some of your income into certain retirement accounts (more on this in Chapter 28), you do not pay income tax on the amount which went into your retirement account (this amount is referred to as pre-tax dollars). Instead, you will pay an income tax when you withdraw money from the retirement account (hopefully, this is after you retire and not before). So, you are still taxed, but the taxed is deferred to a later time.

The advantage to this is that most people will pay a lower tax when the money is withdrawn from the account. Why? It is because in most cases, your income will drop when you retire, which puts you into a lower tax bracket. For instance, say you are in the 30% tax bracket before retirement but drop to the 15% tax bracket after retirement. This means the amount of money you now pay in income taxes is significantly lower. Heck, the government gets enough of my money, so I am going to take every advantage I have to keep my money!

Here's an example. You retire with a million dollars in your retirement account. The money continues to grow during your retirement, and you withdraw some of that money each month to live on. (Remember, you may no longer work, but your money is still working for you!) You pay income tax on the amount you withdraw, so over the next 20 to 30 years, you can potentially pay taxes on 1.5 to 2 million dollars. Lowering your income tax from 30% to 15% could be a tax savings of $150,000 or more! You will need that extra money when you are no longer working and on a fixed income!

Even if you did not start saving for retirement at an early age, it's not too late! Many people think that because they did not contribute to a retirement account when they were young, it is too late. They believe they are doomed to work past normal retirement age. So, they continue with their normal spending patterns, thinking their future is set, and thinking they will have to work until they die. Fortunately, you CAN find ways to plan and save for your retirement even as you get older. The later you start contributing, the higher the percentage of your income you will need to put into your retirement account. By increasing the amount of your regular contributions, you can in effect "make up" for the lack of contributions in the past. It means that you may have to tighten the belt and cut back on expenses. In some cases, you may have to cut back for only a limited amount of time; it depends on your age and how far behind you are with savings. Once you get to the point where you should be money wise with your retirement account, then you can make adjustments to your spending and saving rates. Initially, there will be some sacrifice, but your future is on the line. It is worth it!

I know someone who is a perfect example of this. She had been married twice, and both husbands both had big financial problems. Both were financially irresponsible. Husband number one had a gambling problem. He spent money which had been set aside to pay the bills, and he emptied their joint savings account. Husband number two had a spending problem. He actually liquidated their retirement account and bought a boat and an RV! He tossed credit card statements and collection notices into the trash without opening them! Creditors called day and night. The situation was so bad with husband number two that although they continued to live together and by all appearances were man and wife, my friend legally divorced her husband in order to protect herself financially and to salvage her credit rating.

Eventually, this marriage ended, too. In her early 40's, my friend had lost everything, including her retirement savings, not once, but twice. Starting from ground zero, she was determined to get back on track financially, including saving for retirement. She lived frugally and saved hard. She used credit cards only for convenience and paid the balance each month. To avoid paying interest on a loan, she saved up for a car and paid cash. When she got a higher-paying job, she did not change her lifestyle; instead, the extra money went straight into her retirement account. Not only did she get her finances back on track, she retired early at age 59.

Oh, by the way – this friend is my wife! It helps tremendously that we are both on the same page about finances and living within our means, and we both stepped up our retirement contributions at a late age. We had a common goal and embraced the frugal lifestyle. When you work as a team, reaching the goal is so much easier. If you are working against each other, you may be prevented from EVER reaching your goals.

So, take it from us. Even if you get a late start, you can still reach your goals. Even if early retirement is out of the question, plan so that you may retire while you are still young enough and healthy, so that you may enjoy it. It's never too late to save and improve your situation!

Why Save Money In A Retirement Plan?

After you retire, Social Security is rarely enough to live on. You will need additional money to survive. Saving for retirement will help you to accomplish this. Some say, "I will just save on my own for retirement." I do encourage this, in ADDITION to participating in the retirement plan offered at your workplace, if there is one. There are many reasons to participate in a structured retirement plan. In some cases, an employer will match the amount of money an employee puts into the account, often 2% to 4% of the employee's gross wages. ("Gross" wages are the wages earned, before taxes and other deductions are taken out). For example, if you contribute 3% of your wages to your retirement account, your employer will contribute the same amount to your retirement account. This "free" money doubles each contribution to your retirement savings. You would be well advised to take advantage of this offer. When looking for employment, it may be a good idea to look for an employer whose retirement plan includes contribution matching.

Another reason to participate in a retirement plan is to take advantage of tax incentives. As stated above, some retirement plans allow you to put money into the account BEFORE it is taxed by the government, and the money is not taxed while it is growing through stocks, bonds, mutual funds, etc. The money (income) is taxed when you withdraw money from the account during retirement, usually at a lower tax rate.

Risk Tolerance Based on Age

So, how much risk should you take with your retirement investments? It depends. Factors to consider are your age, how much you can afford to lose if investments don't go well, and how close you are to retirement. Remember my story about older folks who made high-risk stock market investments, and then the market crashed. People who were close to retirement had to delay their retirement, some indefinitely, because they lost so much of their retirement money. Sometimes, their problem was greed. Many dreamed that they could have more money to spend when they retired, IF they would just take a chance and invest in the latest stock fads. Dreams of fantastic vacations, new cars, and vacation homes enticed people to invest in high-risk investments even though they were close to retirement age. Unfortunately, when the stock market tanked, so did those dreams, along with dreams of early retirement.

High-risk investments are investments which typically have a higher possibility of high returns (make money) if the stock market does well; however, they also have a higher possibility of losses (lose money) if the market does not do well. Low-risk investments are investments which typically have lower returns if the market does well, but they also typically lose less money if the market does poorly.

The reason to adjust your investments based on age is that if your investment loses money when you are younger, you have a number of working years to recover from the losses. On the other hand, if you are close to retiring, you may not have enough working years left to recover from a heavy loss. With lower-risk investments, you usually have lower returns (don't make as much money), but you reduce the chance of losing all of your retirement money.

Usually, equities (stocks) are higher risk. Investments such as bonds, certificates of deposits (CDs), money market savings accounts, treasury bills, and stocks of large successful corporations with reliable track records of stability have less risk.

Generally, those who are younger can have higher-risk investments, and then gradually change to increasingly lower-risk investments as they get closer to retirement. A rule of thumb is to subtract your age from 100, and this will tell you what percentage of your retirement savings you should invest in stocks. For instance, if you are 35 years old, then 65% of your retirement savings should be invested in stocks. If you are 60 years old, then only 40% of your savings should be invested in stocks. This is based on a retirement age of 65.

"I fondly remember the time
before the money ran out."

401(k)

A 401(k) is a retirement savings plan sponsored by an employer. It is a common type of retirement account offered by large companies. Money is taken from your paycheck before taxes (matched by your employer if you are lucky) and deposited into a retirement account with one of many financial firms such as Fidelity, Lincoln, AIG, VALIC, etc. Most will have representatives who will help you with your investments, or you may use their website and choose which "products" you want to invest in yourself. Most companies limit the choices of your investments (typically, you may have more choices with a traditional Individual Retirement Account (IRA)). Most 401(k) plans invest in various mutual funds which include a mix of stocks and bonds. Some are made up of USA companies, some of foreign investments, and some a mixture of the two. You are typically given choices of investment products, and you can base your decision on what to invest in based on your age and risk tolerance. You have the option to change the percentages of high-, medium-, and low-risk investments based on your situation (e.g., as you get closer to retirement).

403(b)

A 403(b) retirement plan is similar to a 401(k), but it is available to employees of hospitals, public education organizations, self-employed ministers in the United States, and some 501(c)3 non-profit organizations.

Pension Plans

A pension is a type of retirement plan where the employer contributes money to the plan while the employee is working. In some cases, the employee may also contribute to the pension fund. There are several differences between a pension plan and the plans described above:

- A pension plan is funded by the employer. 401(k) and 403(b) plans are funded primarily by the employee.
- A 401(k) or 403(b) allows the employee to have control over the contributions, but a pension plan does not.
- 401(k) or 403(b) often yield higher returns than a pension plan; however, a pension plan guarantees a monthly check of a particular amount upon reaching retirement age. A 401(k) or 403(b) does not have a guarantee of a return or an amount. Since you control the risk and reward, you also control the amount of the return.

Many governments (e.g. federal, state, county, city) have pension plans for their employees. But, because governments are running out of funds to support these pensions, pension plans are becoming more rare. Contributing factors are that retirees are living longer than the financial planners had figured, expenses have risen to higher than anticipated, and returns on investments are lower than projected (look at the current low interest rate). Pensions are also popular with labor unions.

Pension plans have different formats. One format is that the amount of pension received depends on how long an employee works for the company. For instance, if you work for the company for 20 years, you might receive 50% your normal salary; if you work 30 years, you may receive up to 70% of your salary.

Another example is that an employee would be paid $100 per month for every year of service. So, an employee who worked for the company for 30 years would receive $3,000 per month. This is why you see government employees, such as firemen and policemen, work for 20 years and then retire. They receive their pension and find full- or part-time work in another field.

Be aware that if you retire early, the amount of your monthly pension payments will be reduced if you choose to receive the payments early. For example, the terms of my pension plan states that an employee will received the full pension if he or she receives payments starting at age 65. If the employee chooses to collect the pension before age 65, he or she will receive a 5% reduction for each year prior to age 65. So, if an employee retires ten years early and wishes to start collecting the pension right away, he or she would have a 50% reduction in the monthly pension payments. In most cases, you may choose to retire early but not receive payments until you reach the age where the full pension will be paid.

Social Security

"I wonder if this will effect
our Social Security checks."

Yes, Social Security is essentially part of a retirement plan. To be eligible for Social Security benefits, you must have worked at least ten years at a nongovernmental job and pay into the Social Security system. Benefits are based on your earnings. There are four types of Social Security benefits: Retirement, disability, dependents, and survivor benefits.

Social Security is funded by the employee and managed (some say mis-managed) by the Federal Government. Participation by employees of certain employers is mandatory. On your paycheck stub, one line in the "FICA" (Federal Insurance Contributions Act) category states the amount which is deducted from your paycheck and sent to the Government to fund Social Security.

Some people say that Social Security is an "entitlement". This is not the case, because recipients pay into the Social Security system. This is our money and is not an "entitlement" such as Welfare or other government handouts. My family received survivor benefits after my father's death because he had paid into the Social Security system. He never personally saw the money, but his family did. (Survivor benefits helps families of widows and widowers. My father died when I was two years old, and Social Security survivor benefits helped my mother keep the house where I grew up.) Most Americans pay into the system starting when they are young, working in gas stations and fast food restaurants, and throughout their life. We can only hope that the Government will protect the Social Security funds so that they are available when our children retire.

The amount you receive from Social Security is determined by how much money you earn during the entire time you work and when you start receiving the benefits. This makes sense. The Government deducts a percentage of your paycheck for Social Security, so the bigger your paycheck, the more you pay into the system. If you pay more into the system, you should receive more when you retire. Currently, someone who pays into Social Security earns one "credit" for every $1,300 paid into the system, up to four credits per year. When you earn 40 credits (a minimum of ten years) you become vested and are eligible to receive Social Security when you reach retirement age.

For retirement benefits, you may choose to receive Social Security payments any time after reaching age 62. Currently, the full-benefit retirement age is considered to be 66 years and two months for those born between 1943 and 1954 or earlier, and gradually increases to age 67 for those born in 1960 or later. As an incentive to hold off on receiving Social Security payments, the monthly payment will be incrementally higher for each year you wait past age 62 to receive benefits, up to age 70. These increases max out at age 70.

Social Security retirement benefits continue throughout your lifetime. Some say that in the end, you will receive the same amount of money whether you start collecting lower monthly payments starting at 62 or larger monthly payments starting at age 70, but that is not always the case. I did the calculations for myself. If I live to the age of 85, I will receive around $90,000 more if I wait until age 70 before claiming my benefits. But who knows if I will live to age 85? If I die at age 75, the total dollars received will be greater if I receive benefits starting at age 62 rather than age 70. On the other hand, if I planned to collect Social

Security starting at age 70 but die at age 66, then I would get nothing! It's a crapshoot. A big guessing game that few know the answer to is, "How old will I be when I die"? Sometimes you can estimate based on your health and family history, but you never know for sure.

If you and your spouse are both eligible for Social Security benefits and one of you dies, the surviving spouse is eligible to receive the higher of the two benefits. If you are a non-working spouse and your spouse dies, then you are eligible to receive your spouse's retirement benefits once you reach the eligible retirement age.

To give you an idea of how much (or how little!) money we are talking about, I will give you my personal social security projected income. These projections are based on the age at which I may start drawing benefits. If I start taking benefits at age 62, my monthly benefit will be $1,378. If I wait until age 67, my monthly benefit will be $1,634. If I wait until age 70, my monthly benefit will be $2,026. Could you live on this amount of money? If not, then all the more reason you need a supplemental retirement plan.

Now for the bad news. Some fear that the Social Security system will run out of money by the time some of us need it, especially for those who are younger. For this reason, you should not depend on it. Participate in your company pension, 401(k), or 403(b) retirement plans, or open an Individual Retirement Account (more on IRAs below).

There are several reasons that the Social Security system may not be sustainable in the future. One is that the system was put into place many years ago, and things have since changed. People live longer now than in years past, and the system did not plan for this. As time goes on, the amount in paid benefits will exceed the amount paid into the system. Not only that, but the U.S. Government has "borrowed" from Social Security funds.

The Government's ability to pay future Social Security benefits is unsure. Funds collected for Social Security do not go into an account designated only for Social Security. Instead, the funds go to the United States General Treasury. When money designated for Social Security is used ("borrowed") for other purposes, this affects the future of the Social Security system. The system depends on the financial health of the United States and the ability of the Government to pay back the "loan". At the time of this writing, The U.S. government is close to 30 trillion dollars in debt; repayment of this national debt seems impossible.

Individual Retirement Plans

Individual Retirement Account

Nothing says you can't save for your own retirement if a retirement plan is not offered by your employer. An Individual Retirement Account (IRA) is a retirement savings account available to individuals and provides tax advantages for retirement savings. Initially, IRAs were available only to those who were not covered by an employment-based retirement plan, but today anyone can have an IRA. Investments held in IRAs include stocks, bonds, exchange-traded funds (ETFs), mutual funds, and many other investment options. There are several types: Traditional IRA, Roth IRA, SEP IRA, SIMPLE IRA, Rollover IRA, and Conduit IRA. Due to current tax laws, Rollover and Conduit IRAs are now considered obsolete.

Individual taxpayers have Traditional and Roth IRAs. Small business owners and self-employed individuals use SEP and SIMPLE IRAs. You may contribute to an IRA with earned income that meets IRA rules.

We will talk here only about Traditional and Roth IRAs. These are self-directed IRAs, which allow investors to make their own decisions and have access to more diverse investments, such as real estate, private placements, and tax liens. Here are some, but not all of the differences between the two. Note that rules are subject to change, so always check the current rules when opening an account:

Taxes:

Roth: Contributions are made with money after income taxes have been taken out of your paycheck. The advantage is that when you withdraw from a Roth IRA upon retirement, you do not pay taxes on the money you withdraw. Tax savings can be substantial if your investments grow a lot.

Traditional: Contributions are made before your employer takes out any payroll taxes out of your paycheck. You therefore do not pay income taxes on the money you contribute (tax deferred). Income taxes are paid when funds are withdrawn from the account, similar to a 401(k) or 403(b).

Withdrawal of contributions (money you put in):

Roth: Withdraw anytime, with no taxes or penalties on the money you initially invest.

Traditional: If withdrawn before age 59 ½, the money is taxable and subject to penalties.

Withdrawal of earnings (the money earned by the money you put into the account):

Roth: If at least age 59-½ and the account has been active at least five years, there is no tax or penalty for withdrawals.

Traditional: If before age 59-½, withdrawals are taxed and subject to penalties.

Age restrictions:

Roth: None
Traditional: During the tax year of a contribution, you must be under age 70 ½.

Eligibility:

Roth: Must have U.S. earned income. You may contribute only with certain filing status, and your Modified Adjusted Gross Income (MAGI) does not exceed specified amounts (meaning, if you make too much money, you may not be able to contribute to an IRA).

Traditional: Must have U.S. earned income. No restrictions on contributions.

<u>Required Minimum Distributions (RMDs):</u>

Roth: None
Traditional: Must begin taking distributions the year you turn age 70-½.

Chapter 30
Can I Afford to Retire? Figuring it Out.

Create a Retirement Budget

Once again, we will talk about creating a budget. Now that you know how to create a budget (Chapter 12), you have the tools needed to attain your financial goals. Retirement should be one of these!

Determine Your Fixed Retirement Expenses:
- Groceries
- Car Payments
- Auto Insurance
- Gasoline
- Car Maintenance
- Mortgage
- Rent
- Association fees (if applicable)
- Home Insurance
- Property Taxes
- Utilities (water, electricity, garbage pickup)
- Cell Phone Bills
- Cable and Internet access
- Other Loan Payments (education loans, home equity loans, etc.)
- House Maintenance
- Alimony or other support

- Health Insurance. If you have health insurance through your employer, costs will change when you obtain health insurance on your own. Determine which insurance plan is best for you, based on your health situation and what you can afford. For example, if you are a diabetic, make sure you can get the health care and medicine you need, at a price you can afford. Remember, your health condition can change at any time, more so the older you get.
- Medicare. Most are eligible for Medicare at age 65 (some with a qualifying disability are eligible earlier). The cost can be deducted from your Social Security check.
- Other healthcare expenses. Know that healthcare costs will increase as you get older, including the annual deductible, co-pays, prescription drugs, and items not covered by insurance. Costs will vary depending on your health, age and other determining factors like smoking.
- Extended-care insurance (For a facility like a nursing home, Medicare only covers a limited number of days)
- Consider obtaining secondary insurance to cover things not covered by Medicare. For example, if Medicare pays for 85% of a hospital stay, you can purchase additional insurance from one of the major insurance companies to cover the other 15%. Online calculators are available to help you determine the cost of supplementary insurance.
- Any other expenses

Determine Your Variable Retirement Expenses:
- Vacation costs
- Gifts
- Clothes
- Dining out
- Misc. credit card charges
- Personal "Stuff" like hobby expenses
- Any other expenses

Determine Expected Future Expenses:
- Car replacement
- New roof on the house
- Repainting the house
- Home maintenance and upgrades
- Plumbing maintenance and upgrades
- New air conditioning/heating unit
- Education tuition for kids or grandkids
- Elective surgical procedures (like hip or knee replacement)
- Computer and/or phone replacement (becoming more of a necessity than a luxury, especially if you have not upgraded in a long time)
- Miscellaneous items (only you know what these are)

Now, figure out which costs can be reduced or eliminated. You have the most control in the "variable" categories. For instance, you can change how often you go out to eat or buy new clothes or "toys". Take a hard look at your credit card statements and determine what you NEED to buy versus what you WANT to buy. What can you purchase that will cost less but still meet your needs? Did you really need that new designer wardrobe or the latest and most expensive smartphone? My smartphone is an Android phone which I bought at Costco. I paid less than $200 for it, and it does everything as well or better than my old iPhone, at a fraction of the cost.

Once you work out the variable costs, estimate the cost of future items and look for ways to reduce costs for these items, as well. Use the internet to do research. Ask knowledgeable friends and relatives. Get creative!

<u>Calculate Total Estimated Expenses:</u>

Finally, total all your expenses to determine your estimated annual expenses.

Now, you need to calculate for inflation. You should expect your expenses to increase an average of around 2.5% every year. This rate can go up or down, so use this only as a reference for estimate purposes. For example, based on a 2.5% annual inflation rate, an item you purchase today for $100 will cost over $110 in five years, and over $210 in 30 years ("over" $210 because the increase is compounded on the previous years). Online retirement calculators are available to help you to determine how much you will need to save, based on factors such as your age, life expectancy, how much you expect to receive from Social Security and other retirement accounts, and other factors. Be aware that these calculator programs guess your annual expenses based on a national average. Certain areas of the United States have higher expenses and some have lower. If you do your own calculations, your results will be more accurate (provided you remember all your expenses).

If you want to calculate for inflation on your own, multiply the amount of your total annual expenses by 0.025 (for 2.5% inflation rate). This will estimate increases due to inflation for the following year. Then do the same for each year, multiplying the new amount obtained for each year by 0.025. Calculate a new "adjusted-for-inflation" amount for each year of your life expectancy. This will give you a more accurate estimate for total cost of your expenses over the years.

Example:

First year:	$50,000 estimated annual expenses
Second year:	$50,000 x 0.025 = $1,250. $50,000 + $1,250 = $51,250 estimated annual expenses
Third year:	$51,250 x 0.025 = $1,281.25 $51,250 + $1,281.25 = $52,531.25 estimated annual expenses

Here is an example over ten years:

Year	Expense	2.5% Increase	New Total
1	$59,170.00		$59,170.00
2	$59,170.00	$1,479.25	$60,649.25
3	$59,170.00	$1,516.23	$62,165.48
4	$59,170.00	$1,554.14	$63,719.62
5	$59,170.00	$1,592.99	$65,312.61
6	$57,118.00	$1,632.82	$66,945.42
7	$57,118.00	$1,673.64	$68,619.06
8	$57,118.00	$1,715.48	$70,334.54
9	$57,118.00	$1,758.36	$72,092.90
10	$57,118.00	$1,802.32	$73,895.22

Total estimated expenses for ten years: $662,904.10

Note that a 2.5% increase each year, due to inflation, adds up. After ten years, the original annual expense of $59,170 eventually grew to an annual expense of $73,895. This is substantial! Expenses increase about 1.4 times the original amount in 15 years, and double after 30 years.

Determine how many years you expect to live after retirement (see below for more on this). Calculate the "New Total" for each of those years. For example, if you expect to live ten more years, then the chart above with ten years is sufficient. If you expect to live 40 more years after retirement, calculate a New Total for each of 40 years (if you know how to use a computer program such as Excel, the computer can do this for you). Add the amounts in the New Total column to determine how much you will need for your full retirement (again, a computer program such as Excel makes this easy!). Some graph paper and a calculator can do the same thing. Write this amount down, as it is important.

Determine Your Retirement Income:

First, make a list of all your income and assets:
- Amount in your savings and checking account
- Projected income from savings accounts
- Amount in your retirement account(s)
- Anticipated income on retirement accounts
- Cash you have on hand
- Amount you have in any brokerage accounts holding stocks or other investments
- Social Security benefits
- Value of any property you own or any other valuables which are relatively easy to sell, such as collectible coins, gold, silver, luxury watches, etc.
- Income from stock dividends, alimony payments, rental property, etc.
- Any other income

Next, total all the income and write this amount down.

Now, calculate the number of years you expect to live after you retire. Currently, life expectancy is about 81 years for women and 76 years for men. If you retire at age 65 and expect to live to age 85, you need to make sure you have enough to live on for at least 20 years. Adjust your life expectancy based on your health and family history. For example, if your parents and grandparents live into their 90's and you have a healthy lifestyle, there is a good chance you will live longer than the national average. On the other hand, if you have health issues, your life expectancy may be less. Once you estimate the number of years you will live in retirement, use this to calculate the amount of money you need to have saved or in your retirement accounts.

It is always better to be conservative in your estimates. It's better to have money leftover when you die than it is to run out of money when you need it most in your latter years.

Calculating Income from Retirement Accounts:

Estimating the amount of income you expect to receive from retirement accounts and other investments can be difficult, as there are variable gains and losses which you cannot always predict. Remember, when you retire, you want to invest conservatively. If you don't invest conservatively, you risk losing a large chunk of your retirement and may have to go back to work! At the time of this writing, a reasonable, conservative return is around 5%. The closer you get to 10% and above, the more you increase your risk. Calculating the income on your retirement investments also changes as you start withdrawing money from the account. How much you withdraw will depend on your individual budget and expenses.

Below is an example on calculating retirement income growth. For simplicity, this example will have only one withdrawal for annual expenses at the beginning of the year. In reality, you would likely have several withdrawals throughout the year.

Example:

1. You have $500,000 in retirement savings
2. You withdraw $30,000 at the beginning of year one for expenses. This leaves $470,000.
3. At the end of the year, you have a 5% return on the $470,000, which means you earned $23,500 on your investment. ($470,000 x 0.05 = $23,500)
4. Add the $23,500 to $470,000, and you now have $493,500.
5. For year two, you withdraw $30,750 for expenses (2.5% more than year one, due to inflation). $493,500 minus $30,750 leaves you with $462,750.

6. Another 5% return that year is $23,137.50, which increases your account total from $462,750 to $485,888.
7. Repeat these calculations for every year that you expect to be retired. This will give you your estimated retirement savings balance for each year, adjusting for expense withdrawals and earnings.
8. Your actual withdrawal amounts will vary, depending on your particular situation.
9. The amount earned on your investments will vary and is determined by the type of investments, which are generally defined by the degree of risk. Higher risk, higher returns. Lower risk, lower returns. Once again, higher-risk investments could also mean greater losses, where lower loses are associated with lower-risk investments.

Here is the above example in table format

Start Amount	$500,000.00
Beginning of year one: Withdrawal for annual expenses	-$30,000.00
Amount remaining after withdrawal ($500,000 minus $30,000)	$470,000.00
Return rate for year one	5%
Earnings ($470,000 times 0.05)	$23,500.00
Amount remaining after year one earnings ($470,000 plus $23,500)	$493,500.00
Beginning of year two: Withdrawal for annual expenses	-$30,750.00
Amount remaining after withdrawal ($493,500 minus $30,750)	$462,750.00
Return rate for year two	5%
Earnings ($462,750 times 0.05)	$23,137.50
Amount remaining after year two earnings ($463,000 plus $23,137.50)	$485,888.00

To determine whether or not you have enough to retire, subtract the amount of your expenses from your total projected income. If the result is a positive number, congratulations! You have enough money to retire. It is important to be conservative here. Make sure you have a buffer; that is, make sure you will have enough money to cover unexpected expenses. If you retire with only enough money to scrape by with normal expenses each month, you will be in trouble when unexpected expenses arise.

If the result is negative number, keep saving! Continue with your "goal budget" until you have enough to retire. To determine how much more you need to save before you can retire, divide the amount you need to save by the amount you are able to save each year. This number is the number of years before you can afford to retire:

Total amount you need to save =   Number of years before you can retire
Amount you can save per year

Example:

After determining all your retirement expenses (including a buffer for unexpected expenses) determining your retirement income and creating a budget the for the number of years you expect to live, you see that you need to save another $100,000 before you can retire. You also determine that you can save $20,000 per year (before you retire, that is).

$100,000 total needed   = 5 years
$20,000 needed per year

You need to save for five more years before you can retire.

Remember, this is all estimate work. Many things can change. Inflation can change. Your health can go bad. You or a family member may experience a catastrophic life event, such as an illness or an accident, which will completely alter your calculations and change your financial future. Nursing homes are extremely expensive and can alter financial situations drastically. As you recall, my mom was in a nursing home for almost five years, at a cost of $84,000 per year. Luckily, she had extended-care insurance, which covered 40% of her costs until she reached the $125,000 policy limit. Even with extended-care insurance, her out-of-pocket cost was $259,000 over the five years. If she had not had extended-care insurance, her out-of-pocket would have been $384,000. Her medications alone, AFTER the insurance companies paid their share, cost her $1,000 per month.

Remember, too, that retirement incomes are calculated at different rates by different institutions, depending on the investment type. Also, your expenses may vary year to year, especially medical expenses. Expect your medical expenses to increase as you age and know that there is no way to predict your future health. So, future expenses are an educated guess at best. One of the best things you can do to better your chances of being healthier in your retirement years is to take better care of yourself today! Eat right, exercise, stop smoking and cut down on your alcohol consumption.

Advice for Those Who do Manage to Retire Early

"Don't move, there's a bee on your back."

My friend who retired in his 40's gave me some really good advice shortly before I retired:

- People will have different reactions to your success. Some will be congratulatory, but in general, people your age or older who are still working don't like to hear that you are retired. They wish they were in your position, but they are not and may never be. So, be prepared to feel some resentment, jealousy, and envy (one of the seven original deadly sins).
- If you are able to do any side work, tell people you are only semi-retired unless you want to get into a long conversation. People want to milk you for information about how you were able to retire early while they cannot. They want to know if there is some special secret that they don't know about. Sometimes, you may feel like talking about it, but most of the time you do not.
- Be mindful of your friends' work schedules. Don't call working friends during the week to see if they can do some activity with you, as they still

have jobs and most likely cannot. They will be resentful and will say, "Dude, some of us still have to work!". It's easy to forget what day of the week it is when every day is like Sunday.

- You will notice how busy you are and wonder how you were able to do it all when you had a job.
- Sleeping in is a great option, but you will find that you will not do it often because there is too much to do. The difference is that now you can do things you want to do instead of things you have to do.
- You will see friends driving new cars they get every two years, or showing off a new truck, boat, house, or home addition. They get all the latest toys and go on great vacations but have no money saved. All this while you and your spouse pinched pennies and drove the same car until it was ready for the scrap heap. Some of these friends are doomed to work forever, and there is nothing you can do to help them, as they don't make an effort to plan for retirement. (One of the reasons for writing this book is to help those friends and family, hopefully before it is too late.)
- Spur-of-the-moment travel is now possible (Last minute cruise discounts!).
- Resist the urge to make a lot of "easy" money by investing in high-risk investments and business opportunities; otherwise, you may lose it all and have to go back to work!
- It can be lonely if you don't have a great partner to share retirement with because others your own age are still working. The only people that can relate to you and your situation are often years older, and they don't want to do the same activities that you do. (You may want to go skiing and the older group may be content in their "book of the month club".)
- Successful people will rejoice for you. Those who are confident will embrace your accomplishment. On the other hand, others will shun you and make excuses for their inability to achieve the same accomplishment; they will ignore your years of hard work and planning, investing, strategizing, and sacrifice.

If you are a collector of "stuff", ask yourself, "How much of this do I really need?". Sometimes collecting is a form of mental illness. We have all heard of "hoarders", people who collect things to the extreme, and their homes are so crammed with "stuff" that they are able to walk only in narrow paths in their homes.

There are many good reasons why you should not collect too much stuff:

- Contrary to popular belief, the person that dies with the most toys does not win. You will create a big giant headache for your family after your death, as they will have to figure out how they are going to clean up your mess and get rid of all your "treasures".
- Some rent a storage unit to store all their stuff. I have a friend who rented a storage unit for 25 years. He realized that he had spent $50,000 in rental fees! After 25 years, he went through the space and threw everything away. This was $50,000 of wasted money; it could have grown to as much as quarter million dollars if he invested the money instead.
- How many _____ (fill in the blank) do you really need? I took a decluttering class once and got some good advice. If you have multiple items which are the same and can afford to buy a replacement if needed, then get rid of the extras. Every year for Christmas, my in-laws gave me a pair of sweatpants and a sweatshirt. I would wear only one set for five years or so till it wore out. After 15 years, I had a whole box of brand-new sweatpants and sweatshirts with the tags still on them. I finally gave away all except two pairs. Ten years later I still have the second pair.

One technique is to hang all your clothes hangers backwards in the closet (with the clothes on them). Whenever you wear something, place the it back into the closet with the hanger in the normal position. After one year, look at all the hangers that are still in the backwards position; they are clothes you haven't worn in more than a year! Get rid of items you never wear. (Don't wait for the clothes to come back into style; they will only look good on those 30 years younger than yourself!)

- At a certain point, hopefully sooner than later, you will figure out that a lot of the stuff you buy, you really don't need. Don't waste money that could be saved for retirement.
- People often buy stuff not because they need it, but because "it was such a good deal!". Don't purchase items just because it was on sale or because it is cheaper in large quantities unless you know FOR SURE you are going to use it in a timely manner. A "great deal" is not a great deal if you don't use the item. Recently, Costco had my favorite bourbon on sale for $10 off the 1.75-liter jug. I bought four bottles! I know that they won't go to waste. (I would have bought more if I had a place to store it.)

So, How Did We Manage To Retire Early?

Regarding our ability to retire early, friends often ask "How did you do it??". The answer is that we followed everything in this book. Here are some examples:

- My wife and I both received college educations and found jobs which allowed us to be able to "afford" to save money.
- We live in a very modest home in an affordable neighborhood. At under 1,000 square feet, it is one of the smallest homes on the block.
- Paying off the mortgage was our number one priority, and we worked hard to pay it off early. Now the house is paid for, and we have no

monthly mortgage or rent payment. Mortgage or rent is often people's largest monthly expense; it is also where they pay the most interest (unless their credit cards are out of control). The sooner you can pay off your mortgage, the less interest you pay. The money you save can be invested and used to make money.

- In addition to a lower purchase price, a small house has other financial advantages. Property taxes, insurance, and maintenance cost less. We have low utility bills (much less to heat and cool). Tiny houses are all the rage now, and for good reason. They are a great way to reduce costs.
- We are on a voluntary plan with our electric company, Southern California Edison (SCE), where SCE can shut off our air conditioner during peak electricity use times. Yes, we can be a bit uncomfortable when this happens; however, it happens only two or three days a year, and the savings is considerable. Our electric bill is rarely greater than $50 per month. Our friend who has a large house in Alaska pays as much $8,000 per winter to heat his big house!
- We pay off our credit card bills in full each month. If we can't afford to pay the bill in full, we don't make the purchase.
- While working, we chose to have as much as possible deducted from our paychecks, to go directly into our retirement accounts. We kept enough money to allow us to pay the bills and do fun things, but our modest lifestyle allowed us to save more. If money is deducted directly from your paycheck, you get used to living on a smaller paycheck and don't even notice the money is missing after a while. Then, sit back and watch the balance in your retirement account grow.
- We own modest cars. We both drive relatively inexpensive Honda sedans; they are reliable, with low maintenance, fuel and insurance costs. They are nice to drive with all the basic creature comforts.
- We keep our cars for many years, a minimum of ten years and usually closer to 15 years. We also own a truck to tow our travel trailer; it is over 20 years old. It has a diesel engine, and mileage-wise, it is just broken in, as diesel engines last a loooong time.
- I do all the maintenance on the vehicles, which saves a ton of money.
- We do all the maintenance on our house, including plumbing and electrical (I am a handy guy; she is a handy girl).
- We enjoy a good restaurant meal but eat most of our meals at home. (Fortunately, we love to cook. Why pay a bunch of money when I can cook a gourmet meal at home at a fraction of the cost of a restaurant meal?)
- We shop at discount grocery stores. If Costco sells something we use, we buy it there because the savings are usually substantial. We buy items in bulk only if we are sure to use them. We buy meats in bulk, and then cut them up into smaller portions and freeze them.

- My wife does all the gardening and landscaping herself. She landscaped the front yard with a low-maintenance, drought-tolerant design (yes, drought-tolerant can be colorful and beautiful!), to save money on water and maintenance.
- We go on an occasional cruise or other vacations, but most vacations are in our RV. We love camping, and it is significantly cheaper than a luxury vacation. Many state park campgrounds cost as low as $12 per night. The RV has a full kitchen, so we save money by cooking our meals, and we eat very well. The savings of taking RV vacations over traditional luxury vacations means the RV will pay for itself over time. Also, RV's are also a great mobile disaster kit, which could come in handy one day since we live in earthquake country.
- We were lucky in that the timing of our stock market investments was good. I pulled all my money out of stocks in 2008 just prior to the major market crash and avoided the big loss that many others suffered. Yes, there is some luck (good and bad) involved when investing in the stock market; I was lucky in this case.
- We had some good stock picks on companies which did well, such as Netflix and Amazon, and made good returns on our money. We are avid customers of both companies and therefore invested in what we like and understand. Yes, there was some luck involved here, too.
- Neither of us is a big shopper. We buy what we need and rarely indulge in luxury items. We do own nice things but don't make a habit of buying such items often. We save for items and pay cash so that we don't pay interest on a loan or credit card. My wife buys most her clothing at discount stores, and I am really lucky because she doesn't like expensive jewelry! I am a jeans and T-shirt kind of guy and hate wearing suits and ties. (Designer clothing is uncomfortable to me. Plus, I regularly stain my shirts with food since I love to eat! Not a problem when I spend $10-$20 for a shirt versus $75 for a nice dress shirt.)
- I am a computer guy by profession and do all our computer repairs, upgrades, network maintenance, etc. myself.
- We bundled our cable and internet at a substantial savings. To save money, we had our telephone land line disconnected when we retired. To save more money, we "cut the cord" and installed a roof top TV antenna; we now use cable for internet access only, since Netflix and Amazon have a bunch of great content.
- We keep our smartphones and other electronic devices until they don't work anymore. We don't upgrade every time a newer version is released.
- My wife and I get along really well, so the best times we have is spending quality time together. We don't need to spend a lot of money on material items or expensive vacations. Spending quality time together does not mean you have to be anywhere special or expensive; it just means being

together doing something we both enjoy. We have been on some really fantastic vacations, but we budgeted for those vacations and paid for the vacations only AFTER money was set aside for bills and retirement savings.

So, it is not any one thing that enabled us to retire early; it was a combination of many things. Living within your means is a lifestyle. Anyone can embrace this lifestyle if they have the will and discipline. Spending a lot of money is not a prerequisite for happiness.

My wife and I learned many skills over the years so that we could save money by doing things ourselves rather than hiring someone else to do it. You, too, can learn! There are many resources available, such as books, classes, and the internet. YouTube is an amazing source when it comes to learning how to do something. The money we saved by learning these skills was a large factor in allowing us to retire at an earlier age. You would be surprised at what you can do it if you put your mind to it.

We hope that we set a good example for our children and that they learn from us. Together, we have three children, and fortunately, they all have good financial values. They know the importance of good grades and hard work. After graduating college, my daughter worked and saved $100,000. With the help of a scholarship, she paid her own way through graduate school, earned an MBA from UCLA, and was on the Dean's List. She now has a great job. My wife has two sons. They also worked hard and are now a neurologist and an occupational therapist. All three kids are doing well financially. We are lucky; none of them has asked us for money since graduating college. None were "boomerang kids".

Interesting Ramification of Higher Education

Let's start this by saying we are advocates of higher education. Remember the story at the beginning of this book about my boss who said that the only way to afford to save money is to get a high-paying job, which is made possible by higher education. A better-paying job will actually ALLOW you to afford to save money.

I will share an interesting story about a doctor I worked with. He and I are the same age. He is a medical doctor who also has a Ph.D.; this means he has two doctorate degrees. When talking to him about my upcoming retirement, he told me he would love to retire but cannot, and he was envious of me. In order to obtain those advanced degrees he spent many years in college. If I had to guess, I would say he probably completed college when he was 30 to 35 years old. After becoming a doctor, he started a family and became a father in his late thirties. He now has two children. Compare this to myself. I have a four-year degree, graduated from college at age 23, married, and became a father at age 25.

My doctor friend has a beautiful big house in an affluent Southern California neighborhood. He and his wife drive expensive imported cars. Their children go to the best schools and are close to college age. If he wants them to have the same education opportunities that he had, he is looking at paying for six to eight years of college for each child. In today's dollars, this can be $300,000 to $500,000 per child or more, so he may need a million dollars to pay for his children's' education. Since he already has a lot of debt from a big house, luxury cars, and getting his degrees, it will be difficult to save a million dollars to pay for the kids' education. In addition, due to his income level, his children will not qualify for any financial aid.

I started saving for my daughter's college education the day she was born. She is now in her early 30s, her education is paid for, and she is financially independent. If my doctor friend had done the same, and IF he had lived a frugal lifestyle with a modest home and modest cars, he probably could have saved a million dollars for his kids' education and retire five years earlier than I did. Unfortunately, many people spend more if they make more, not thinking about the long-term benefits of living frugally and saving for the future. To most, early retirement sounds like an unobtainable dream rather than a possible reality.

Working in the medical field for 30 years, we know many doctors who work not for the money, but instead are on a mission to help people. They love their work and make huge impacts in peoples' lives. We know doctors who worked well into their 80's because they loved their work and because they wanted to fulfill their mission of helping others. On the other hand, we also know doctors who only went into medicine because they wanted to make good money. Since their heart is not into their work, they are miserable. They don't like working long hours and getting calls in the middle of the night. Today, the costs of doing business in the medical field are increasing, while reimbursement from insurance companies is decreasing. Young doctors who went to medical school with dreams of becoming rich are coming out of medical school deeply in debt and finding the that the money they expected to make is not there. It will take many, many years to pay off their education debt. Little did they know!

All this being said, obtaining an advanced degree CAN assist you in your goal to retire early, but you must be careful that the cost of education does not place a financial burden on you that you cannot pay back in a timely manner. Make sure when you spend a lot of money for an education, that it is in a field which has good employment opportunities. It is interesting that the extra years my friend spent in college adversely affected his ability to retire early, because he started a family later in life and increased his spending when he had an increase in salary. He also reduced his income earning years because he was in college for an extended period of time. He wants to retire but is far from his financial goal.

It is our hope that if you are reading this, you can alter your spending and savings habits as early as possible, so that you may reach your goals later in life, regardless of your education level.

Chapter 31
Wills, Probates, and Trusts

Wills, probates, and trusts can be complicated and often require more information than this book can provide. Here we will go over only the basics.

Wills:

A will is a legal document that specifically describes how a person (the "testator") wishes to distribute property (both real and personal property) and assets after their death. A will can also name an executor, name guardians for children, create trusts for children or other beneficiaries, forgive depts, and more.

There are many types or formats used, but a will must meet legal requirements. Most wills are formal documents which are signed and dated by the testator and two witnesses who won't benefit from the will. It is best to have a will notarized by a notary public; this is an authorized person who verifies the identities of those who sign a document and who witnesses the signatures. The document is then marked ("sealed") with a special stamp. Depending on the state or jurisdiction, sometimes a handwritten will without witness signatures is acceptable; however, these may create more difficulty after death of the testator. The person who makes a will must be an adult who has the capacity to understand what they are doing when they make the will. If your will is simple, there are good self-help products available which can help you to create a will without an attorney. However, if your situation is complicated, it is best to hire a qualified professional.

Even if you distribute your property through a trust or other estate planning tool, you should have a will. If you die without a will, state laws will decide who inherits your estate.

<u>Probate:</u>

Probate is a legal process where a judge gives legal permission for assets to be distributed to heirs, whether or not there is a will. During the legal process, a will is proven (verified) to be the true last testament of the testator and accepted as a valid document by probate court. In the absence of a legal will, probate is used to settle the estate according to state laws.

A probate court verifies the information in the will, identifies outstanding debts and liabilities of the estate, and verifies the title of any property owned. A title must be verified before it is transferred or sold to any heirs named in the will. It is typical that outstanding liabilities are paid before money and property are distributed to heirs. In some cases, probate court will require that property is to be sold to pay outstanding depts before assets are distributed.

The probate court works with the executor of a will; this is the person who has the legal power to distribute assets and carry out the testator's wishes as defined in the will. Ideally, the executor is designated in the will. If no executor is designated in the will, or if the designated person declines the responsibility, the court will appoint one. After a will is verified and outstanding claims are resolved, the probate court grants its approval (that is, grants probate) to the executor. When probate is granted, the will is considered "probated" and legal, and the executor becomes official. If a person dies without a will, a legal representative is determined by the court and is called an "administrator" rather than an executor.

Probate can cost tens of thousands of dollars and take a year or more to resolve. Probate laws vary from state to state. Most states allow small estates to go through a simplified process which does not require a probate attorney. With careful planning, it is possible to avoid probate. Avoiding probate can reduce legal fees, avoid estate taxes, and protect privacy. One of the best ways to avoid probate is to create a revocable living trust (more information below). Some retirement or pension plans, life insurance policies, and medical savings accounts are not subject to probate.

There are complicated legal and tax processes involved with probate. Having a will makes it easier for your loved ones in the event of your death. In more complicated cases, it is best to work with professionals (an attorney and a financial advisor) to make sure that you don't leave a mess for your heirs.

Trusts:

First, let's define the word "fiduciary". A fiduciary is someone (or an organization) who acts on the behalf of someone else to manage assets. A fiduciary is expected to act in good faith (trust) and to carry out fiduciary duties in an ethical manner.

Now, we'll explain trusts. A trust is a fiduciary relationship where a "trustor" (the person who funds the trust) gives a "trustee" the right to hold title to property or assets for a third party or parties (the trustor's beneficiaries). A "beneficiary" is someone who is named to receive a share of the trustor's assets and/or property in the event of the trustor's death. In other words, the trustees hold onto and protect the trustor's assets, to make sure those assets are distributed to beneficiaries according to the trustor's wishes.

A trust is created by drafting a legal document and is usually made with the assistance of an estate attorney. Rules and restrictions regarding trusts vary from state to state. Costs vary, depending on the complexity of the estate, but for most, a trust can usually be created for a few thousand dollars. The trustor(s), trustee(s), executor(s), and beneficiaries are named in the trust. Creating a trust can allow heirs to avoid probate or make the probate process easier, faster, and less expensive. It may also allow beneficiaries to avoid or reduce inheritance or estate taxes. A few thousand dollars to create a trust may seem like a lot to some, but it will save your loved ones a lot of time, headaches, and money.

There are different types of trusts, which fall into six main categories: Living (also known as an inter-vivos) or testamentary (also known as will) trusts, revocable or irrevocable trusts, and funded or unfunded trusts.

Only certain types of trusts will protect money and property from lawsuits. An asset protection trust or a properly drafted irrevocable trust are two examples of trusts which can provide asset protection. In general, revocable trusts do not provide protection against lawsuits. The most common type of trust is a revocable trust. With a revocable trust, the trustor can more easily make changes to the trust, including changing beneficiaries. On the other hand, an irrevocable trust cannot be easily revoked, changed, or amended. Changes can be made only by the designated trustee. This trustee usually cannot be a spouse, close relative, employee, or agent of the trustor. This difficulty in making changes is one of the things that protects an irrevocable trust from lawsuits and creditors.

Here is an example of asset protection with a properly drafted irrevocable trust. If you are in an accident and seriously injure someone, money or property in the trust cannot be taken from the trust in a lawsuit. As the trustor, you may fund the trust, but only the trustee has control of the money and property in the trust. With an irrevocable trust, you no longer own the money and property. The trust has ownership; this is why it is legally protected from a lawsuit against you.

Remember, the above information on wills, probates, and trusts only covers the basics. Remember, also, that laws vary from state to state. There is much more information available; be sure to do research and obtain professional help, if appropriate.

Chapter 32
Bankruptcy

Bankruptcy:

If you follow the advice in this book, hopefully you will never get to the point where you will need to declare bankruptcy. So, what is bankruptcy? It is a legal process which allows a person or business to be relieved from debt. The person or business who owes money is the "debtor". If a debtor is unable to pay outstanding debts, the debtor may file a petition in a federal court, requesting freedom from the debts or finding a way to repay the debts.

The person or business who you owe the money to is the "creditor". Bankruptcy can also allow an opportunity for a creditor to receive payment. In some cases, a debt will be dismissed, meaning you don't have to pay it back; however, in other cases, a debt is restructured so that you can repay it over a period of time, or you may be required to sell property to help pay off the debt. Debts may also be reduced. Bankruptcy may allow a fresh start, but it also has some downsides, which we will talk about below.

There are several types of bankruptcy. The most common types are known as "Chapter 7", "Chapter 11", and "Chapter 13".

Before we talk about different kinds of bankruptcy, I will explain the difference between "secured" and "unsecured" debts.

A secured loan is a loan which is attached to a physical item, such as a house or a car (this is collateral). If you are unable to repay the loan, the lender may repossess the item. Collateral helps to guarantee the loan. It means the lender takes less of a risk, so interest rates on secured loans are lower.

An unsecured loan has no collateral. A lender takes a higher risk with an unsecured loan, because if you do not repay the loan, there is no collateral for the lender to collect. The lender may sue you to receive payment, but they cannot take your home or car. Since there is no collateral associated with unsecured loans, you will pay a higher interest rate.

Different Chapters

Chapter 7 Bankruptcy

Chapter 7 bankruptcy is also known as liquidation bankruptcy. It is used when a debtor has few or no assets, and it allows a debtor to dispose of unsecured debts such as credit cards or medical bills. With a liquidation bankruptcy, the debtor must sell (liquidate) certain property to repay unsecured debts.

Chapter 11 Bankruptcy

Chapter 11 bankruptcy is used by businesses, and rarely by individuals. It allows a debtor to reorganize and get back on their feet. With the court's supervision, a business can work out a repayment plan and continue to maintain the business.

Chapter 13 Bankruptcy

Chapter 13 bankruptcy is used by debtors who have too much money to qualify for a Chapter 7 bankruptcy. In a Chapter 13 bankruptcy, an agreement (a "covenant") is reached, which may lower a debt and/or provide a workable payment plan. If the debts are paid, the debtor is allowed to keep their property. Typically, payments are made over a period of three to five years.

Pros of Bankruptcy

- You obtain protection from creditors and avoid repossession of property (such as your car), wage garnishment, and harassment.
- You can protect your home or business.
- Some debts may be reduced or dismissed.

Cons of Bankruptcy

- Bankruptcy can lower your credit rating. This flags you as high risk to lenders and makes it difficult to obtain future credit or loans.
- If you are able to obtain a loan, you may pay a higher loan rate than someone with a high credit score.
- Financially responsible people generally make better employees; therefore employers often use credit ratings as a guide to screen job applicants. A low credit rating could have a negative impact on your ability to obtain employment. The same is true regarding renting a home or apartment. Having a bankruptcy on your record may discourage the owner from renting to you.
- Studies have shown that those with a low credit score are more likely to file more medical insurance claims and have more expensive claims. Due to this, insurance companies will also check your credit score. If the score is low due to a bankruptcy on your record, you may pay a higher premium for health insurance.
- If you have bankruptcy on your record, some companies, such as telephone or utility companies, may require you to pay for services in advance.
- Depending on the type of bankruptcy, it can remain on your credit report for up to ten years, meaning your credit rating will be damaged during this time.

So, the bottom line: Avoid bankruptcy, if possible! Do your best to prevent being in a position where you need to declare bankruptcy. It should be considered as a last alternative, right before fleeing the country! (Just kidding. Fleeing the country to avoid debt is a bad idea! The USA is a great place to live!) Remember, depending on who you owe money to, Guido from the Mafia may find you and say, "I gotta break something, the boss says…"

Pay your debts!

Chapter 33
Loaning Money to Friends and Family

Risks of Loaning Money

Many people at one point in their life are asked to loan money to a friend or family member. Loaning money to friends and family often carries a high risk that the money will not be paid back. If the loan is not paid back in a timely manner or is never paid back at all, this can cause damage, sometimes permanent, to the relationship between the friends or family members. In some cases, the situation may cause a financial hardship for the lender.

A good way to lose a friendship is to loan money to a friend or family member, and then the person does not pay back the loan. If you do agree to loan money, you must make sure that you will be okay if the money is never paid back, both financially and emotionally.

Here are a few examples where this happened to my wife and me:

Case 1:

I first learned this lesson in high school. I loaned a friend some money. As the time went by without receiving my money back, so did my resentment. Eventually, the friendship was ruined. The guy who borrowed the money avoided all contact with me. I'm sure he did not want to run into me so that I could ask "Where is my money?".

Case 2:

I have a distant relative who was always down on his luck financially. Years ago, he asked me for a loan. I knew I would take a risk if I loaned him the money and fully expected that he would not pay back the loan. I wanted to help him but could not afford to lose the amount he requested, so I agreed to loan him a lesser amount. He gratefully accepted the reduce amount. I was okay with the loan because I never expected to get paid back. Over the years, I completely forgot about the loan. Surprisingly, my relative contacted me eight years later to say a check was in the mail, and I received the money a few days later! I never expected to get paid back, so it was a big surprise.

The lesson here is that it was okay to loan the money because I did not expect to get the money back, and I made sure to loan only the amount I could afford to lose. Also, this relative had never asked me for money before. If he had previously requested money from me and taken a long time to repay the loan, I would have denied the request for this reason.

Case 3:

A close family member asked my wife to co-sign on a loan so that he could purchase a car. When co-signing for a loan, the co-signer becomes legally liable for repayment in the event the borrower defaults on the loan. Non-payment can ruin the credit of both parties involved. This family member has a history of erratic behavior and financial problems, and she told him she would not co-sign. The end result of not co-signing on the loan? The family member "disowned" her, and she has not heard from him since. That was over 20 years ago! Remember, this was a close family member. Declining to co-sign for the loan was a wise decision because the loan amount was too great and a financial burden my wife could not afford.

Case 4:

The last family story involves my own father as told to me by my mother. My father owned a gas station and was a mechanic. One of his employees wanted to obtain a loan from the bank and asked my father to co-sign on the loan. My father loved people and always tried to see the good in them, and he was happy to help the employee. Unfortunately, the employee "burned" him and defaulted on the loan, making my father responsible for repayment. The incident really affected my father.

After this incident, my father developed an ulcer which never healed. It literally "burned him up" inside. The ulcer eventually led to stomach cancer, which killed him at the young age of 43. My mother believed that the stress of the loan situation led to the ulcer. Today, we know that his ulcer was likely due to H-pylori bacteria. H-pylori infection is easily treated with antibiotics, but in 1965, this was not known. The stress from co-signing on a loan is what actually killed him indirectly!

Our personal policy now is that if a friend asks for a loan, we will decline. The friend might be angry, but if he is truly a friend, he will get over it, and we will remain friends in the end. On the other hand, if we were to lend the money, and repayment was delayed or never paid, the end result will be permanent damage or loss of friendship. (In the back of my mind, I have considered lending money to "friends" that I would rather never hear from again!)

Lending money to family members may have different conditions. If a family member asks to borrow money, we may grant the request with a different frame of mind, with the knowledge that we may never get paid back. Going in with this attitude, there is less chance of damage to the relationship. You can't pick your family! An occasional loan to a family member is okay as long as you can afford the loss, and as long as the person who borrows the money does not abuse the relationship. If you loan money repeatedly to someone who does not repay the loan, you become and enabler and play a role in perpetuating that person's dependence and irresponsibility.

So, learn from the stories above and be extra careful if you make a decision to loan money to someone.

Get It In Writing

If you do decide to loan money, it is a good idea to put something in writing. My wife told me a story from an episode of "Judge Judy", where there two (previously) close friends had a dispute over non-payment of a loan. The plaintiff was suing because she loaned money to the defendant, but the defendant did not pay back the loan. The defendant claimed it was not a loan; she said the plaintiff told her it was a "gift". Without something in writing, it is one person's word against another.

Not that you would take a family member to court but at least by putting it in writing, there is no misunderstanding that the loan was not a "gift".

Promissory Notes

If you want to make the loan legally binding, you can draft a "Promissory Note", also known as an "IOU". It is a legally binding contract. The promissory note should contain the following:

1. The date of the loan
2. Who the borrower is
3. Who the lender is
4. The amount of the loan

5. The date when the loan will be paid back by
6. If payments are agreed to, the amount of the payments and the frequency (e.g monthly, weekly, etc.)
7. Any interest to be charged (if applicable)
8. Whether or not the loan is secured (by property) or unsecured
9. Whether or not more than one person is responsible for payment (cosigner(s)). If so, each person responsible needs to sign the note. The note need not be signed by the lender.

A promissory note may seem like overkill for a small loan. If you want to make sure there is no misunderstanding and you want to make sure you have legal recourse in court for non-payment, then draft a promissory note. If you really want to make the promissory note more legally binding, take it to a Notary Public and have the note signed there. This certifies the signatures and further reinforces the legal validity of the document should you need to enforce the contract in court. The borrower can't say, "wasn't me that signed that!".

Chapter 34
Taking Money to the Grave?

There is a point at which saving money becomes an obsession, to the detriment of the saver. There are wealthy people who refuse to spend their money and are unhappy. They don't allow themselves to spend money for enjoyment.

Here are couple of real stories:

Story number one: We know of a husband and wife who are quite wealthy and have no children. The husband is a compulsive saver. He has the same mentality as a person who is a "hoarder", but in this case he hoards money. It can be seen as a form of mental illness. The wife asks the husband for things such as clothing or furniture or a trip to visit her family (who live in another country), and her husband denies her requests. The wife feels like a prisoner in her own home and is not allowed to spend money on anything. The husband does not give her an allowance, and he approves any spending. Needless to say, the wife is unhappy. The husband thinks he is happy because he is accumulating wealth, and he won't to part with any of it. He will die a rich man but doesn't realize he and his wife could have been happier if he had learned to spend some of his money. Hopefully, he will die before she does so that she can live a little! It is important to know how much money we truly need to fulfill our needs. Unless you are saving your money for others, such as your family or maybe a charity, what is the point of having so much money if you can't enjoy it or put it to good use?

Story number two: We know a perpetual bachelor who is also quite wealthy. Back in the day when movies were still shot with film, he worked in the Hollywood movie industry developing and editing movie films, where he made a great deal of money. He is one of the foremost authorities on film in Hollywood. He also inherited his family home in southeast Los Angeles. Although he is wealthy, he is now over 75 years old and still drives the same car he drove in high school (cool classic Chevy from the 50's). He never married. He never travelled and saw the world. He lives a very sheltered and compartmentalized life and has no desire to spend his money. He will die wealthy and alone.

The takeaway here is that the ideal situation is to make sure you have enough money to live comfortably throughout your life, but also allow yourself to enjoy life. Since no one knows how long they are going to live, we need to plan for the best-case scenario of living to a ripe old age. It's better to have money and not need it, than to need money and not have it. The goal is to spend your money responsibly and enjoy life to the fullest. Spend time with loved ones. Travel the world. Enjoy your hobbies. Eat good food and drink fine wine. Find a spouse, partner, or friend who you enjoy being with and enjoy life to the fullest. Donate your time and/or money to someone in need. There is a saying that money can't buy happiness but having money can certainly help you to reach your goal of being happy and healthy.

Chapter 35
The Problem of Spoiling our Children

I know about spoiled children because I was one of them. My parents had very little while growing up and wanted their children to experience a better life. They worked hard to provide their family with a good home and wanted us children to have everything we wanted. Unfortunately, it turned out this was to my detriment.

After my father passed away when I was two years old, my mother sacrificed everything for her children. She rarely bought new clothes for herself, and she never bought luxuries for herself. She worked hard so that she could pay the mortgage, put food on the table, and cover all the expenses her three kids could generate.

I am much younger than my siblings. Therefore, I was raised more like an only child and was spoiled. The result of this is that I expected to be given everything I wanted when I wanted it. I thought only about how things affected me and not others. I remember as a child wanting to buy something, and when I was told I couldn't have it, I vividly remembering experiencing emotional pain.

Spoiling children results in children who expect immediate gratification and who expect to get everything they want. They don't respect others and don't have a good work ethic. Then, they grow up into adults who expect the same thing in life. When these adults are immersed into the real world, they find out that they don't function well in society and blame everyone else for why they can't hold a job.

This desire for immediate gratification fuels credit card problems plaguing people today. Many people today don't learn about patience or the fact that is better to work and save FIRST so that they can buy something. Instead, they charge the purchase to a credit card and worry about how to pay for it later. There is little self-discipline in a credit-focused society that does not stress the importance of responsibility.

The same holds true for parents who give their children all the money they want, so that that the children can buy whatever they want, when they want it. These children don't learn the value of money or what it means to work and earn money on their own. As a result, these children spend like there is no tomorrow and don't want to work. When they become adults, they continue to expect that everything be given to them because that's how it's been their whole life. That is, they feel entitled; hence, the term "entitlement generation".

As a parent, it is often easier to give in to your children and give them whatever they ask for. No arguing involved. No resentment. But as a result, no lessons learned. The more difficult thing to do is to sometimes deny a request and instead teach your children to earn the money to buy what they want. It can be difficult, because a child's natural initial reaction is resentment. We've all seen the "If you really love me, you will do this for me" attitude. By always giving in and spoiling a child, you risk creating a non-functioning, non-contributing member of society.

Okay, so you are wondering how I, as a spoiled and selfish child, turned things around. It was the day I became a father. That day, I realized that everything I did was no longer for me. My life was no longer just about me. It was for my wife and daughter. That day I realized that I had the power and responsibility to raise a child who was free of the demons that had haunted me while growing up.

I also for the first time came to understand the sacrifices my mother had made my whole life. I thanked her for that after becoming a father myself. Up until then, I did not appreciate all that my mother had done and the sacrifices she had made. My mother told me that she brought us into the world, so raising us was her responsibility, and she took her responsibility seriously.

In addition to becoming a father, I was lucky to have other things in my life that helped me to find the right path. One was my martial arts training (which continues to this day, 40+ years later). Through martial arts, I learned self-discipline and to respect others, and it helped me to learn the value of hard physical work. Another was that my first wife was in the financial services industry, and she taught me a lot about investing and money management. So, over time, I acquired the desire, the knowledge, AND the discipline to succeed. One is little good without the other two.

The takeaway here is that it's important not to spoil your children. To succeed in life, we must teach them the skills to work hard, so that they are able to take care of themselves and others.

Chapter 36
Dealing With a Partner Who is Out of Control

Most people do not have a perfect relationship with their spouse, partner, or significant other. Remember how opposites tend to attract? In many partnerships, one partner may have spending habits under control, but the other partner may not. It does little good if one spends two dollars for every dollar the other saves.

Remember the story of my current wife and how she divorced her previous husband to legally protect herself from his out-of-control spending? Without her knowledge, he took money from their retirement account to buy a boat and a motor home even though they were nowhere near retirement. This was only one of many similar incidences regarding their finances. Legal divorce was the only way that she could protect herself from financial ruin. They continued to live together (maybe a little less harmoniously after the boat and motor home incidents), but it took the drastic measure of a divorce to solve a financial problem which could have been avoided with self-control and discipline.

Being a compulsive shopper or spender is sometimes actually a symptom of a mental or emotional issue. If this is the problem in your case, then perhaps you or your partner/spouse need to seek professional help from a counselor or psychologist. On the other hand, if this is not the case, then perhaps logic and reason can work.

For example, say your partner purchased a new dining room set and a new wardrobe, and paid for them with a credit card. Over the next year, the two of you paid $1,500 in interest on the credit card payments. Sit down and have a discussion with your partner. Talk about how you could have saved $1,500 by saving the money before making the purchases. Yes, it will take some sacrifice, patience, and discipline.

Next, record the costs of all miscellaneous charges, such as going to the movies or out to eat or that wonderful daily coffee. You may find that when you record costs over a month or two, those little $5, $10, $20, or $30 expenses can really add up. People don't realize just how much money they actually spend when spending just a few dollars here and there. Before we bought our first house, my first wife and I kept track of all these little expenses so that we would know how much house (debt) we could afford. I was shocked by how much we spent on the little things.

Discuss financial goals with your partner. Talk about how you both can change spending habits. Talk about the importance of working TOGETHER to achieve your goals; make it a team effort. To succeed in becoming financially independent, it is critical that both partners are committed and that you support each other.

Envision together what life would be like if you had no debt. A mortgage that is paid off and credit cards with a zero balance each month. Think of all the money you could save and the things you can do if you have no debt. Having no debt is life changing and is a cause worthy of changing your spending habits.

When my wife and I paid off our house, we budgeted for fun and travel, and we bought some things we had wanted for some time, but only AFTER we added money into our retirement accounts each month. Being able to have fun and purchasing things you want is important, but they need to be part of the budget. Remember, it's easy to get into debt but hard to get out of debt. Kind of like gaining and losing weight!

Work together toward a happier and more stress-free and fun-filled future, by controlling spending and budgeting for a debt-free life.

Chapter 37
Mistakes Made When Suddenly Having a Lot of Money

"I think I just solved my cash flow problem."

You many think the problem of suddenly having a lot of money will never happen to you, but I know some people that this happened to, and they were not prepared to handle it.

Case 1:
I had a coworker and friend who never had much money. Although he and his wife had regular jobs, he also had odd jobs on the side to make ends meet. When his wife died of cancer at an early age, he received $40,000 in life insurance money. He had never had that much money in his life. He told me about the insurance money and said to me, "Man, Rod, I got this money! I always wanted a Chrysler 300 luxury sedan. I'm going to buy it now that I have the cash. I never had this much money in my life! I've always wanted that car and now I can afford to buy it!"

I had a talk with him and told him that he has a rare opportunity here. Maybe once in a lifetime for him. A chance to get ahead. I told him that he could invest the money or use the money to start a small business. Either way, he had a chance to make that $40,000 work for him to get himself ahead. If his small business was successful, he might even get wealthy as a result. If he invested the money in stocks, he could turn that $40,000 into $100,000 or more.

What did he do? He bought the car.

His desire for material things and lack of discipline outweighed common sense. As a result, he likely will be working those extra odd jobs to make ends meet for the rest of his life.

This is an example that if discipline and common sense are not exercised, the loss of financial opportunity is almost certain. Short-term desires can easily destroy long-term opportunities for financial freedom.

Case 2:
Back in the very early days of the California Lottery, people who purchased lottery tickets did not choose their own numbers. Instead, you would purchase a "scratcher" ticket, where you scratched off a covering to reveal hidden numbers or the words "Big Spin" underneath. If three numbers on the ticket matched, you won that amount. Usually, the winnings were only a few dollars, but if you were lucky, you would get three Big Spins. Those who had tickets with three Big Spins got to be on a weekly television show and spin a large wheel, for a chance to win the big money. On the Big Spin, you could win as much as a million dollars.

I knew someone who purchased a ticket and got three Big Spins. He participated in the Big Spin, and he and his wife won $50,000. It was not a million dollars, but it was a lot of money to them. They used the money to put a down payment on a nice new condominium. Both husband and wife had relatively low-paying jobs. Unfortunately, it turned out that they could not afford the mortgage payments and other costs associated with the condo. In the end, they lost the condo and the $50,000 down payment. Due to a lack of basic financial knowledge, they bought more house than they could afford, and it cost them the $50,000.

This case is not unusual. There are many similar stories of lottery winners or others who unexpectedly received a large amount of money. They squander the money, or the money causes much disruption and unhappiness in their lives.

Cases 3 and 4:
I have a friend who has never had much money. She recently retired, lives in an apartment, and lives a very simple life. I also have an aunt and uncle who are in their nineties, are retired, and live in a nice home. In both cases, family members recently passed away and left them with large amounts of property and money.

After the deaths of both her stepfather and mother, my friend inherited their estate. Now, she is dealing with a great deal of stress because she has never dealt with large sums of money and doesn't know what to do. All of a sudden, she has this huge responsibility. The stress is taking a toll on her health. Fortunately, she knows she is in over her head and hired a professional to assist her with settling the estate; however, the stress continues to have a negative impact on her life.

My aunt and uncle are in a similar situation. They are in their 90's and already financially stable, but now they are responsible for settling the estates of not just one, but of two family members who recently passed away. Again, this is creating a great deal of stress for them.

Usually, it's the lack of money which causes of many life problems. Here are cases where too much money causes stress, anxiety, and health problems.

Again, it is true that money can't always buy happiness. As you can see, sometimes having a lot of money can result in stress, unhappiness, and health problems.

Financial freedom is a very powerful thing. It allows you to dictate the terms of your own life instead of bending to the whims of banks and creditors. It provides freedom from debt and debt-related stress, which in turn has positive effects on your mental and physical health. Financial freedom also gives you the flexibility to find a job that you enjoy rather than working at job you don't enjoy but need to keep. It is liberating to know you can walk away from your job if working conditions are bad or your boss is a jerk. With proper planning and discipline, financial freedom will allow you to live better and provide the ability to have the things you want and do the things you enjoy, within reason. It takes budgeting, discipline, and the drive to work. We hope the information in this book helps to educate you on how to take control of your financial life, and through this to have a happier, more FUN, and more enjoyable existence, both today and in the future. The only life that we can be sure of is the one that we live in now. We can't change the past, but we can make the future better.

Don't just exist. Plan, save, and enjoy. Have fun and LIVE!

About the Authors

Rod Kuratomi retired at age 54 from his job as a laboratory systems analyst and clinical safety officer for a Southern California hospital, where he worked for over 29 years. He attended UCLA and California State University at Los Angeles and has a BS in Criminal Justice Administration. Rod is also a seventh-degree black belt and has taught karate at the International Karate Association for more than 35 years. He and Cheryl are both Zen practitioners, and now financial evangelists.

Cheryl is a retired clinical microbiologist and worked in major clinical laboratories for 35 years. She is a graduate of California State University Northridge, with a BA in biology and chemistry. She is a third-degree black belt karate instructor. Cheryl volunteers for the Phil Simon Clinic Tanzania Project, where she is the secretary and treasurer and is on the Finance Committee. Rod and Cheryl have three children and five grandchildren.

Rod and Cheryl have zero debt and own their home and vehicles free and clear. Their goal is to teach others how to be debt free through education, exercising financial discipline, and utilizing planning and budgeting tools to attain financial freedom.

The Kuratomis have travelled all over the world for pleasure and to teach martial arts. They also do volunteer medical work in Africa with the Phil Simon Clinic Tanzania Project. They believe life is too short to retire at an old age or when you are no longer able to enjoy life. Their hope is that you will start planning now so that you may enjoy the freedom to live the life you want to live.